Sober Women and the Power to Choose

Getting Back Your Power and Freedom

Mary J. Wright, RN, MSN

© **Copyright 2023 - All rights reserved.**

The content contained within this book may not be reproduced, duplicated or transmitted without direct written permission from the author or the publisher.

Under no circumstances will any blame or legal responsibility be held against the publisher, or author, for any damages, reparation, or monetary loss due to the information contained within this book, either directly or indirectly.

Legal Notice:

This book is copyright protected. It is only for personal use. You cannot amend, distribute, sell, use, quote or paraphrase any part, or the content within this book, without the consent of the author or publisher.

Disclaimer Notice:

Please note the information contained within this document is for educational and entertainment purposes only. All effort has been executed to present accurate, up to date, reliable, complete information. No warranties of any kind are declared or implied. Readers acknowledge that the author is not engaged in the rendering of legal, financial, medical or professional advice. The content within this book has been derived from various sources. Please consult a licensed professional before attempting any techniques outlined in this book.

By reading this document, the reader agrees that under no circumstances is the author responsible for any losses, direct or indirect, that are incurred as a result of the use of the information contained within this document, including, but not limited to, errors, omissions, or inaccuracies.

Table of Contents

INTRODUCTION 3

CHAPTER 1: A STRUGGLE WITH THE FIRST STEP 9
    WHY SOBRIETY MATTERS 11
    NOT FOR EVERYONE 13
        Binging and Sobriety 13
        A Woman's Experience 14
        Take the Best From the "Big Book" 15

CHAPTER 2: TYPES OF POWER FROM A WOMAN'S PERSPECTIVE 17
    POWER AND CONTROL 18
        Negative Power 20
        Powerful Positives 21
    WHAT DOES POWER HAVE TO DO WITH SOBRIETY? 23

CHAPTER 3: THE POWERLESS MIND 25
    POWER AND THE BRAIN 26
        Short-Term Euphoria 26
        Long-Term Damage 28
        Modeling Power 29

CHAPTER 4: TRANSFORMING OLD HABITS 31
    CLINGING TO OLD HABITS 32
        Habit Identification 33
        Making a Plan 36
        Asking For Help (Yes, It's Okay!) 38

CHAPTER 5: DRINKING AND SEXUAL ASSAULT 41
    MY ALCOHOL-FUELED LIFE 41
    A "FUN" NIGHT OUT 42
    ASSAULT AND ALCOHOL 43
    PRESSURE AND POWER 44
    THE IMPACT OF ASSAULT 44
    WHAT CAN BE DONE? 45
    PREDATORS IN UNEXPECTED PLACES 45

CHAPTER 6: THE BENEFITS OF POWER AND SOBRIETY 47

POWERLESS TO ALCOHOL 48
THE OBVIOUS.. 49
   Brain Health... 49
   Body Health 50
THE NOT-SO-OBVIOUS 50
   Relationships 51
   Self-Esteem 51
   Attitude and Positivity 51
   Life 52
WORKING ON YOURSELF 52

CHAPTER 7: CREATING LASTING BOUNDARIES **55**
WHAT ARE BOUNDARIES?... 55
   Your Needs First... 56
   Relationships and Communication 58
   Break Ups and Forward Movement.. 59
   Boundaries for Peace.. 60

CHAPTER 8: POWER ACHIEVEMENT UNLOCKED! **61**
GET TO KNOW YOURSELF 62
   Power and Support... 63
   Professional Help.. 64
   Decide Who You Will Be 64
   Writing Your Plan 65
   Setting and Resetting Goals 65

CHAPTER 9: A WOMAN'S GUIDE TO VALUES AND PRIORITIES **67**
THE OLD WAYS 68
THERE'S A NEW LEADER IN TOWN.. 69
FORGET WHAT YOU KNOW... 70
PRIORITIZING YOUR SOBRIETY.. 71

CHAPTER 10: ACTIONABLE POWER **73**
IT'S TIME FOR SOMETHING NEW 73
   Calming the Mind 74
   Learn From the Past 76
   Take Your Time 76

CHAPTER 11: SETBACKS AND RESTARTS **79**
A GOAL REMINDER 80
LOVE YOURSELF 82
HELPFUL EMERGENCY SUPPORT 83
KEEP MOVING FORWARD 84

CHAPTER 12: MAINTAINING AND SHARING POWER WITH WOMEN EVERYWHERE 85
    WOMEN UNITE! 86
    POWER OVER YOURSELF 86
    POWER OUTSIDE OF THE HOME 87
    MAXIMIZE YOUR SOBRIETY 88
    KNOW YOUR WORTH 89

CONCLUSION 91
    WHERE ARE YOU NOW? 92
    LONG-TERM INVESTING 93

REFERENCES 95

This book is dedicated to everyone who is suffering at the hands of alcohol and to those who want to stop drinking but find it difficult. May you find a solution that brings you health and happiness.

Introduction

There it was again—the mention of the word "power." As I sat in my Alcoholics Anonymous (AA) meeting, I heard the words from the first step of the program reverberate in my head. "Powerless over alcohol." I thought about this a lot at the beginning and then later over the years. This notion of feeling powerless was certainly true, but this was not my first AA meeting, and I had started to notice the repetition of the word "powerless" each time I attended. I was stuck on this idea as a result.

I continued listening to each meeting I attended, but something inside me didn't feel right. During meetings, some AA participants even said they were powerless over everything when discussing the first step regarding sobriety. Really? Everything? This idea didn't make much sense to me because I didn't feel powerless over *everything*, even though the idea of drinking haunted me. After all, I was at a meeting, and I obviously wanted to take the initiative to stay sober. I didn't understand why this idea of having no power at all had to be part of our conversation. I was afraid to say anything because my attendance at AA was, in fact, helping me remain sober for the first time in my life. Still, at every AA meeting, I couldn't help but secretly think, *If I have no power, how could I survive?*

You see, just a few weeks before I started attending AA meetings, I was seriously contemplating suicide. Trigger warning: If you are in any way having suicidal thoughts, seek help immediately, as there are assistance and professionals who want to help. In my case, I was still yo-yo-ing back and forth with my sobriety. I had tried quitting drinking on my own many times but always ended up in the same beer-filled spot. At work, I'd cover my beer breath daily with gum or mints. At home, I focused on caring for my children as best I could since they were my life. Yes, I always felt a heavy guilt weighing on me because of this. I knew I wasn't being as attentive to my kids as I could be if I were sober. Every day was hard, and it was at this time that I hated myself so much that I'd often think about committing suicide. The idea of leaving my children held me back from doing this, though. I was worried that I'd never be able to quit, and I had countless days and nights when I felt desperate for this to change. Finally, the thought of improving my personal well-being for my children pushed me to attend my first Alcoholics Anonymous meeting. Like so many individuals with a drinking problem, I was convinced that AA would just give me another temporary solution until my next drinking bender. I absolutely didn't want to go to a meeting, but I was desperate to quit and kept thinking of my young children, who needed a sober mother.

In weighing my options, I also feared what an AA group would actually look and feel like. I had only seen depictions of groups like this on television. In my mind, I was worried that I'd have to sit in a circle on a folding chair in a dank classroom or auditorium and be forced to share shameful stories of my drinking. I wasn't ready to share such personal elements of myself with total strangers. Also, I was raised in a religious household, but I didn't want spirituality to dictate my sobriety, so I wasn't confident that a group encouraging a relationship with God was going to work for me. Needless to say, I had many doubts.

I soon learned that Alcoholics Anonymous was a comfortable place where I could be myself and share the uncertainties I was experiencing. AA groups rarely sit in circles, and a person can gain comfort and relief during meetings even if they don't embrace the spiritual wording found in some of the steps. During meetings, I heard people share that the idea of powerlessness and spiritual incorporation sometimes felt restrictive for people in these groups but that these weren't requirements for attendance. As we say in the AA preamble, we share our experience, strength, and hope with each other. The group I found embraced anyone who was seeking help and was a welcoming place for me. If you've thought about trying AA or have tried it but haven't found it successful because of the idea of being powerless or because of the spiritual connection, my advice is to try a few different AA meetings, as various meetings have different tones. You may even want to find meetings where there are more women. The bottom line is to find a system or organization that works best for you. Whether it be a scheduled meeting, an online therapy session, a best friend to confide in, or other programs, finding something that you connect best with and discussing your steps to sobriety is paramount to making it work for you.

In my AA group, I found that any individual could say just about anything they wanted to say during a meeting and that their words would stay protected. After all, this is one of the main tenets of the group. For me, this was also one of the most appealing aspects of the program since I needed a safe space that was free of judgment if I was going to heal. Because those around me could share their stories, fears, and goals, I started discerning what positive takeaways I could gather and what advice from others should be adjusted for my path. I quickly learned that I needed to explore the idea of power more for myself since I had heard some conflicting information from others at these meetings. As I worked through my sobriety, I started journaling more about the idea of power and what it meant to have a lack of it. This topic fascinated me since I was starting a personal exploration of how power impacted my life. I found that, by quitting drinking, I was taking the most important step I could reclaim power in my life. While journaling, I thought back on the years and realized that other pivotal moments in my life also encouraged this power, such as the birth of my children and my divorce from an abusive spouse. Eventually, through a deeper understanding of my situation, I gained a sense of freedom.

Realizing that I had been cultivating power and motivation for myself, I started understanding that I could be a better parent, friend, co-worker, partner, and person. While I'm eternally grateful for the Alcoholics Anonymous program and for what I've learned from it, I also believe that AA is not the only form of recovery treatment for a person struggling with sobriety. I had this power in me before, during, and after my recovery; I just needed some help bringing it to the surface. A part of me felt a deep desire to share my experiences and my journey with others since there is much more to sobriety than the need to start from a powerless position. At certain points in life, a person may feel stuck or low on energy for making changes, and this may, in many ways, feel like a powerless situation, but it doesn't have to equate to this. Change is possible if a person keeps moving forward with their sobriety. By gaining hope, goal-setting, and seeking support from others, a person can grab the personal power they seek.

Pursuing and obtaining sobriety has felt life-changing for me as a woman as well. My definition of what power means to me helps me adjust my attitude and ideas each day. While this book is written from my perspective, that of a woman who sought and achieved sobriety, my experience can educate anyone who seeks help with becoming or remaining sober. My story involves a damaging relationship, a mother's love, and personal growth that I couldn't have done without the support of others. In sharing my experience, I'd like readers to understand how they can take this information and make changes that fit their lives in an effort to achieve long-term sobriety.

Ultimately, my desire is to think about how the wording of the first step of AA works best for me and perhaps others, especially women since this wording could be limiting and even detrimental if it is misunderstood. While the idea of being powerless over alcohol is valid, it's important to understand how a woman may experience this idea differently from a man. I want to promote hope and encourage people who are on the spectrum of Alcohol Use Disorder (AUD) to seek a system that works well for them so that the idea of long-term sobriety is not just a dream but also a reality.

Realize that any steps toward sobriety are the right ones for you. This book will not criticize or judge your journey and won't force you into any situations that you're not ready for. Rather, it will provide guidance, leading you to make your own beneficial choices in life. As encouraged in the tradition of Alcoholics Anonymous, I've chosen to use a pen name, Mary J. Wright, to describe my personal journey. Later, when you're ready to share your experiences with others, you may find that anonymity also serves you well in releasing the fear of feeling judged by others. My personal stories (and they will get personal) will hopefully serve to give you the comfort that you're not alone and can make changes to your life, even when this feels virtually impossible.

In the following chapters, you'll have a chance to understand more about the types of power that hold us back or set us free. For women, traditional ideas of power are changing, and we need to understand our changing values, habits, and goals in society. Each chapter will emphasize a necessary discussion centered around power and the way we can achieve lasting success with sobriety when we know how this power can be used positively.

While I feel that I've lived many lives, it's important to say that my best life has happened during the last 33 years while I've remained sober. As you learn more about my story, consider your life years from now when you can tell your own story of success, whether it be written or verbal. I'm still here today because I learned to harness my power and believe in myself, and you can do the same.

Chapter 1:

A Struggle With the First Step

I was 16 years old in 1971 when I had my first drink. A stranger had bought a group of us some cheap wine at a liquor store, and when I picked up the bottle for the first time, I felt like so many others do as new drinkers of alcohol. Before this day, I had seen hundreds of depictions of people drinking in movies and on television, making them look cool and sexy. Like so many first-time drinkers, I longed to feel this way too. When I drank with my girlfriends that night, I instantly felt more grown up, popular, and attractive, like the stars I'd seen in my favorite scenes of movies. It didn't dawn on me then that Hollywood creates these fictional sequences, and that society continues to buy into their falsity. There have been many societal changes since the 1970s, but one thing remains the same: The perception that drinking will aid a situation. It never does.

This night didn't end well for me. I remember not even liking the taste of what I was drinking but doing it anyway because my friends were there, and I wanted to fit in. *Why do so many people do this?* I thought to myself, but I didn't dare say it aloud. After a few drinks in, I experienced my first blackout. There would be many of these ahead of me in my life, but my first one hit me hard since I didn't expect it and felt unprepared. I finally woke up and found myself lying on the sidewalk. I lost all control of my emotions and began sobbing about the death of my father, which had happened three years prior. I felt alone, sad, lost, and embarrassed, but I didn't equate these feelings to the shock that my system had just felt after downing a bottle of wine. Instead, I sat on the sidewalk and tried to compose myself.

Suddenly, I felt a warm hand on my shoulder and heard a voice saying that it would be alright. I looked to my left, and there was a teenager who I didn't really know but was the cousin of one of my friends. It seemed he could tell that I was not okay, so he asked me to sit still, listen to the sounds around me, and breathe. I did.

Surprisingly, this calmed me down, and I was able to return to my reality. When I think back on this night, I see the opposite of a movie scene, even though, at the time, I wanted it to feel magical and beautiful. Nothing was perfect, nothing looked shiny, and nothing felt good until I was able to calm down at the end of the night. A sensible reaction to these events would have been to never drink again, but like so many individuals, I had gotten a taste of this adult situation, and I wanted to experiment with it even more.

I continued drinking throughout high school with my friends, but by this time, I had switched to beer since I had this first negative experience with wine. Did that solve my problems? Absolutely not. With beer, I still experienced blackouts but thought I was more in control of my situation. I wasn't at all. Every single time I drank, I'd experience a few quick minutes of feeling "good," followed by long blackout periods and then a hangover the next day. Did this make me stop? Still no. Drinking with friends continued for me each and every weekend in high school.

Flash forward to my first few Alcoholics Anonymous meetings, where I was still trying to figure out this program (yes, there is much more to explain about my journey from high school to AA, but that is for another chapter). I remember sitting and pondering the first step. The step reads, "We admitted we were powerless over alcohol—that our lives had become unmanageable" (Stevens, 2023, para. 3). I kept rolling the thought of this step around in my mind. I viewed this step with some value, and I wanted to open myself to understanding it since I was sitting in an AA meeting because I was powerless over alcohol. The more I contemplated this step, the more I began to think about the other things in life that I couldn't control. I'm powerless against other people's actions, the economy, the weather, and many other events around the world. But does this mean that *I* am powerless? I didn't feel that this was what this first step meant for me. I also felt that others might be thinking the same thing but were too afraid of judgment to say anything. AA is over 85 years old, after all. How could a program with such a following ever be called into question? (*History of AA | Alcoholics Anonymous*, n.d.) This program was giving me a new confidence that I was starting to feel proud of, but I also felt that I already possessed the power to make a real change in my life since I had worked up the courage to attempt to get sober for myself and my children.

I began researching, reading, and studying everything I could regarding the idea of power and how it can have a hold on a person in society. This idea mattered to me because it gave me a focus for my sobriety. I didn't want to be powerless, and I needed to prove to myself that this didn't mean I had zero power over my life. This research started me on my quest to discover why sobriety mattered to me and why it should matter to other individuals.

Why Sobriety Matters

My guess is that if you grew up in a religious household, you might have experienced the practice of placing faith in something that you weren't able to see, hear, or touch. This concept asks a person to believe and trust that everything will be okay without much solid evidence or facts, yet for many people, their faith is unwavering. Sobriety is very different, of course, from having spiritual faith, but dissimilar in unexpected ways. While an individual's journey to getting sober asks them to recognize that alcohol has some control over their life, sobriety also comes with many tangibles, fact-based realizations that can provide a person with much comfort throughout their journey to stay sober. The facts about what alcohol can and cannot do for an individual are sometimes difficult to absorb because we so often want something to be true. I, for example, wanted it to be true that I could look and feel like a popular and outgoing person when I was drinking alcohol, which was simply not the case. So many of us dismiss the idea of getting sober simply because society doesn't often recognize the problems that drinking can impose on our lives. So, without further ado, here are several hard-hitting statistics about drinking that will help to encourage you to believe that you're doing the right thing by taking the idea of sobriety seriously.

"Worldwide, alcohol misuse and dependence are responsible for 3.3 million deaths per year, 10 times the number of fatalities from all illicit drugs combined" (Frakt & Carroll, 2020, para. 1). Does reading this statistic make people stop drinking immediately? For some, it may put the idea in their heads, but for many, they feel minimal reactions to this. People in certain societies have long confused the idea of drinking with something that should naturally be a part of life. We got home from work and have a drink. It's the weekend, and we want to drink. Something great has happened, and we celebrate with a drink. Something terrible has occurred, and we think we need to drink. It's no wonder that drinking results in so many deaths each year, but for many, this is a statistic they hear, then quickly forget, or block out.

The world of alcohol is a booming business, and it keeps many companies' wealthy. In the United States, for example, it's easy to walk down a city street, watch commercials, or drive by billboards and see casual advertisements for beer, wine, and liquor. These advertisements are ingrained in us from a young age, and we often think nothing of them while subtly getting unhealthy doses of this propaganda, making us think that it's cool or attractive to drink. In addition, alcohol keeps restaurants, concert venues, and sporting events thriving. Simply stated, alcohol has been a staple in society for money-making reasons for decades. While there are no magical ways to stop people from drinking or abusing alcohol, there are many ways that the public can educate themselves about how society can transform their attraction to drinking so that children and young teenagers are better informed about its danger moving forward. Making free resources more widely available for struggling alcoholics is also a must for any community where alcohol abuse statistics continue to climb.

In 2020, *The New York Times* reported that, of all addiction treatment cases, alcohol accounts for the majority and that alcohol has led to a loss of 250 billion dollars in productivity each year, with this cost coming from alcohol's connection to criminal cases, treatments for alcoholism, and imprisonment related to situations involving alcohol (Frakt & Carroll, 2020). Because Alcoholics Anonymous is the most widely known program for treatment, it's no wonder that many individuals turn to it when they feel the desire to become sober. For individuals who struggle with alcoholism, AA provides accountability and encouragement since engaging in group meetings leads to a higher success rate for sobriety (Guarnotta, 2022). Since AA is available in over 180 countries and has been available to individuals since the mid-

1930s, it also makes sense that this program has created such a following over time.

Not For Everyone

Though AA is one of the most popular ways to get support for alcoholism, it's not the only way to get support, and other programs and resources are worth trying since some of the basic ideas and wording used in AA can feel off-putting for some individuals. I have written another book that talks about AA and alternatives to this program. The most important thing is that any suffering alcoholic can find a solution that works for them. Since the steps developed for Alcoholics Anonymous were created long ago and can feel outdated when discussing sobriety today, individuals may be searching for a different form of recovery. After all, five out of the twelve steps mention God and encourage a faith-based approach. This concept may not suit all individuals, especially in modern times when spirituality in some societies may be on the decline. While the steps of AA are designed to help keep an open mindset since this course of action embraces the idea that there is a high power, it also feels like this idea provides individuals with an excuse to relapse. "Rigorous study of programs like Alcoholics Anonymous is challenging because people self-select into them" (Frakt & Carroll, 2020, para. 1). This makes it difficult to truly track the success rate of this program versus other methods of sobriety. The bottom line is that if an organization, friend, idea, or therapist can work to sustain a person's sobriety, it should be viewed as a beneficial factor and one worth pursuing.

Binging and Sobriety

For my life and situation, Alcoholics Anonymous has felt 99 percent successful. I know that many others see it as a helpful comfort when searching for a way to maintain sobriety, but there are outdated and uncomfortable ideas that may feel off-putting when considering the steps that this organization promotes. For some, the idea that a person is powerless against alcohol can contribute to a cycle of falling on and off the "drinking wagon" since this idea doesn't necessarily place a person in complete control of their actions and may give them an excuse to keep binging before returning to sobriety (Glaser, 2015). Of course, the real solution to any drinking slip-up is to never have picked up a drink in the first place, but since most of us don't own a time machine, we need different solutions. Tools for getting and remaining sober can feel old-fashioned in our modern age, so it's important to find or create a plan that works for you regardless of how it works for someone else.

In many cases, to remain sober, it's necessary to mix strategies so that many sources are working in one's favor. For example, attending an AA meeting on Monday, a therapy session on Wednesday, and setting aside time to talk with sober friends on Friday is a plan that could work to encourage sobriety throughout your week. Since accountability is key, planning several moments throughout each week can serve as a vital check-in for ownership of our sobriety. We'll have more moments to explore the creation of a sober plan in later chapters of this book but allow this idea to prompt your thinking in what may become a helpful and encouraging sobriety check-in for you.

A Woman's Experience

Many of us would like to think that a woman's experience during a sober journey would be identical to a man's, but as you may know, this just isn't the case. One of the major differences for women may be their interpretation of the idea of power. Alternative programs, such as *Women For Sobriety*, exist so that communities of women can gather regardless of race, financial situation, or religion (*Women for Sobriety*, n.d.). Transgender women are also welcome to attend these meetings. One of the aspects that this group recognizes is that everyone has a unique situation and story, and there isn't always a one-size-fits-all answer to sobriety. The concept of power differs for women, and when this is recognized by sober groups, specialized care can be developed and provided.

For women, the idea of power is often associated with a certain independence as well. This was true for me, as I spent years in an oppressive, abusive marriage because I thought I had to stay there for geographical and legal reasons. With my divorce came a sense of empowerment like I hadn't experienced before. Alcoholics Anonymous worked well for me because I already had a powerful sense of who I was, and I simply needed help maintaining this. I received this help from the friends and members I met in this group.

Because Alcoholics Anonymous may not work for everyone and, specifically, every woman, it's necessary to find a group that will feel comfortable and brings forth confidence.

Take the Best From the "Big Book"

I happen to have been fortunate enough to have had an amazing relationship with my sponsor from Alcoholics Anonymous. I hold this individual responsible for my ability to remain sober and seek answers to the questions I have been looking for in my life. My sponsor always reflects on the ideas of AA and helps me understand concepts from the "Big Book" instead of simply parroting the words from this book. Created in 1939, the "Big Book" is a textbook that outlines the twelve steps of Alcoholics Anonymous and describes the journey of the first 100 individuals who worked to maintain their sobriety (*The Big Book | Alcoholics Anonymous*, n.d.). This book promotes the idea of remaining powerless so that you can allow the AA program to work, beginning from a vulnerable place. This idea never made sense to me and didn't make much sense to my sponsor, either. This idea of powerlessness over things other than alcohol was hard for me to understand, and I have discussed it at length with my sponsor over the years. She and I spoke openly and honestly about our discrepancies with this idea, and together, we worked to create a hopeful attitude rather than a powerless one. If it weren't for our discussions and seeing ideas from another woman's perspective, I doubt I would have attended more meetings. One of the most admirable things that I learned through our conversations was that it was okay to rethink the major tenets of AA as long as these ideas were accessible to me and promoted my sobriety. I also learned that I wasn't powerless but rather quite powerful every day.

I mention my perspective on AA not to turn anyone away from trying it because this program can be an extremely safe place when alcohol takes hold, but I continue to rethink the ideas of power and sobriety so that I can spread helpful and mindful advice to others who crave long-term sobriety when I meet with them at AA meetings. Just as I "took the best" from the "Big Book," I'd recommend grasping the best ideas that resonate with you as we continue to explore concepts of sobriety and power. There's a popular saying in AA that says, "Take what you need and leave the rest" (LaPierre, n.d., para. 2). This sentence has helped guide me along my path of sobriety for over 30 years, and I feel it can benefit many others as well.

In the next section, we'll continue to examine power as it applies to women in their quest for sobriety or continuing sobriety. By exploring various types of power, we can learn more about personalizing your sober journey.

Chapter 2:

Types of Power From a Woman's Perspective

I was 18 years old in the 1970s and living in a dorm room in Manhattan while attending a university. I was now on my own. At least when I drank in high school, I often felt protected by my friends since I would, in many cases, sleepover at their homes after or while consuming alcohol, unbeknownst to their parents. When I got to college, though, I felt that I no longer had this confined protection within my free range in the city. There were cool clubs and bars that I was going out to now since the legal drinking age in the United States at the time was 18. I had a job as well at this time, so I was making money that could somewhat support this lifestyle. I'd go out each weekend with the intention of only drinking a small amount at a jazz club or music venue, but almost every weekend, I'd end up back at the dorm with my girlfriends, having blacked out until the next morning. Was I proud of this? No! Did it happen often? Yes!

Winding up safely back in my dorm room happened on nights when I was lucky. On other occasions, I'd wake up in strange places, having no memory of how I got there or of whose apartment I was even sleeping in. I'd have vague flashes of talking with guys at bars but never remember going from the bar to a different location. Every night when I went out, I had plans to return to my dorm room, but this only happened about half the time. Everything felt unpredictable and frightening, but somehow, I didn't want to equate the problem with alcohol. Many mornings, I would wake up on a couch in a stranger's apartment or in a luxury hotel and wouldn't be able to find something I had with me the night before, whether it be my keys, wallet, or jacket. I want to stress here that this happened more than once, and I'm sorry to say that I didn't often learn a lesson from my reckless behavior.

At the time, I didn't even feel like I was drinking that much. For me, a night of drinking usually meant two or three beers, which for many people seems like a minimal amount. For me, however, this was blackout territory and the point where I would lose my memory of the evening. One morning, in particular, I awoke in a stranger's apartment and saw handguns on the coffee table that I'd been sleeping near the night before. I left that apartment quickly, only to discover that I was in Alphabet City, one of the most crime-ridden areas of New York City in the 1970s. My dorm roommate was just about the only person who knew my drinking habits, and to them, my drinking problem must have looked scary, but I kept clinging to the dream that I could casually go out each night, have a couple of beers, and end up back at my dorm each time, safe in my own bed. I was so wrong about this notion, as I'd often end up in places that I didn't recognize without having any memory of walking or taking the subway there. This dangerous practice continued, and each time, I naively thought that I'd just go out for a couple of beers, then get back home safe and sound. Every time was the same, though. I'd go out to a bar, have a few beers, then blackout, forgetting major parts of the night, and finally wake up in either my dorm or a stranger's place. I never knew which it would be, and my drinking was placing me on a dangerous course of destruction. I knew if I didn't stop, I'd be seriously harmed or worse, but every time, the thought of drinking "just a few" coerced me back into spending late nights out without remembering most of the conversations or experiences I engaged in. This was my life.

Power and Control

Many of us are taught that having power is a positive aspect of leadership in life, so why should a woman become powerless over alcohol? To answer this, we need to look closer at the idea of power in our society as well as the concept of control. Oppression doesn't lead to success in sobriety and should not be used to exert power over someone during recovery. Additionally, women often face struggles in relationships when power is used for control. After college, I was involved in a 24-year marriage in Spain with a person who also had substance abuse issues and was violent, so I'm familiar with feelings of powerlessness over alcohol as well as feeling powerless in this relationship. More on this later, as I feel it impacted my ability to gather the strength to become sober.

Specifically, in the business world, five kinds of power are often defined. These types of powers, or a lack of them, can often make or break success. In examining these categories, we can see how they can either motivate and encourage or destroy and demoralize. It's important to become familiar with them as well as the positives and negatives associated with power. While we look at these from a corporate lens, consider ways that these may apply to sobriety, and then we'll synthesize this application to make connections to ways that power may drive success or harm a journey to sobriety.

The following are common forms of power used in business and society (Rigby, n.d.):

- **Coercion:** You may have just cringed at even reading this word since coercion is typically associated with negativity. In business, if an employer uses coercion to exert power, they tend to push the rules on employees, making it challenging for any deviation. Some employers may view this as a "tough love" approach, but this form of power tends to result in a poor work environment since employees feel intimidated and forced to obey.

- **Expertise:** This type of power can be challenging to maintain once a person is placed in a leadership position since it relies on the concept that the leader is the ultimate expert. It doesn't make much room for other ideas from employees or growth from a sharing of ideas but rather assumes that the leader is the most knowledgeable and will make all of the decisions.

- **Legitimacy:** Similar in some ways to coercion, legitimacy reinforces the idea that the person in a position of hierarchy leads people who are beneath their position of power since the person in a higher position has been given the power. While this will encourage structure, it will also feel inflexible for growth and movement since individuals may feel stuck in their current position.

- **Reward:** This form of power encourages a person to work toward a goal because they're going to receive a tangible or intangible reward. Whether it be a raise in money, a prize, or just simple praise, some reward hangs over a person and motivates them to work toward achieving it.

- **Referent:** This personal form of power is the one that stands out as a positive system as far as successful forms of power go. With this type, leaders build relationships, trust, and honesty with others so that there is a collaborative working system instead of a hierarchical structure.

Consider what resonates with you about these types of powers. Have you seen these in action, whether in your place of employment or outside of work? How can we recognize when power is helping or hurting us when applying it to sobriety? To answer these questions, let's dive even deeper into categorizing the forms of negative and positive power.

Negative Power

Even though power is typically viewed as a positive aspect in corporate settings, there are times when negative power takes control and is hard to recover from. In these cases, power types such as coercion, expertise, and legitimacy may take hold and leave no room for change or growth at a company. These negative power types apply to our interactions outside of the business world as well since, in social situations, a person who desires control over another person, group, or situation may try to take this power.

While this domineering personality is unlikely to gain much respect in the long run, it can lead to a difficult dynamic between parties. For example, dominating the conversation, interrupting others, or making others feel inferior can make another person feel powerless as they try to navigate social situations. An unequal power struggle arises when an individual isn't given a chance or opportunity to speak, share opinions, or participate socially because of another individual's dominance. For an alcoholic working to become sober, this kind of negative social situation can feel especially dangerous since a person with Alcohol Use Disorder (AUD) is already working to overcome vulnerability.

For a person new to an AA group, hearing the word "powerless" may quickly send a confusing message to them, even if the point of this is to understand that you can no longer try to battle alcohol. Alcohol will win every time. For women, the idea of having power can sometimes be complicated, but on the other hand, the idea of becoming powerless can be a scary message. In the workplace as well as in social situations, a woman who is unapologetically intelligent and knows what she wants can often be viewed as having negative qualities, whereas a man with similar assertive attributes may be seen as a leader. While this is an unfair and unfortunate reality, it should not hold a woman back from pursuing sobriety or from recognizing and highlighting these biased situations. Because I was fortunate enough to know some strong women in AA who helped me understand the idea of power in a way that was different from the wording of the original steps from the "Big Book," I was able to see that I already possessed an amount of power because of my experiences and because of the desire I had to become sober.

Powerful Positives

In many cases, having power will be an asset. Think about it. When we have some kind of control over our lives, this tends to help with goal achievement, motivation, relationships, confidence, and adaptability. In most cases, though, the power needs to feel mutual and comfortable rather than dominant or unequal. From the power types above, we can gather that having referent power is, in fact, the most positive form since this kind creates a working partnership with others. This, of course, can feel challenging in terms of first getting sober because the power may feel out of reach due to the circumstances. Having the support of others is crucial during this stage. When helpful groups or individuals can provide guidance and a non-judgmental ear, a person may make faster and stronger breakthroughs with their sobriety, leading to more confidence in themselves and, ultimately, resulting in a powerful mindset of positivity.

The Power of Habit Creation

Now that we've discussed how important recognizing the power within us can be, it's also helpful to understand that forming habits can make a person feel powerful since habits allow for clearer thoughts and confidence. If you've heard the old adage of "one day at a time," you'll know that this idea gives a person some short-term motivation so that the thought of completing an activity for life doesn't become overwhelming. When you change your mindset from one that values doing something forever to one that simply completes a task by doing it one small amount at a time, sobriety becomes much more manageable. Of course, the goal is long-term sobriety, but for many, this idea can become overwhelming and quickly lead back to a life of drinking.

Typically, powerful people have one important thing in common. They have learned to incorporate achievable habits and make them personal to them, so these habits work with their lives (Bradberry, 2016). These habits help these people work toward success because they remain manageable and because they lead to the end goal of task completion. According to Dr. Travis Bradberry (2016), co-author of *Emotional Intelligence 2.0*, these habits include

- taking action and not waiting to receive a job title or status of some kind to start leading.

- learning methods to stimulate discussions.

- recognizing what you're good at and what you could improve on.

- using courteous behavior to make profound changes (even when the idea is unpopular).

- requesting assistance when challenges arise.

- obtaining and holding onto a network of peers.

- understanding that conflict will happen (get comfortable with the uncomfortable).

- focusing on what matters most.

- independently instead of following the crowd.

- having the belief that success is possible.

- getting to work on goals now!

In terms of applying these habits to sobriety, it's important to keep in mind that becoming and remaining sober does take some confidence, but this is achievable since taking that first step in recognizing that a problem exists is a step in the direction of confidence.

What Does Power Have to Do With Sobriety?

I realize that saying a sense of powerlessness doesn't have to be a part of the path to sobriety may sound strange since I'm not newly sober, and for me, the start of my sobriety happened years ago. I still feel that I can offer hope to anyone struggling to begin their journey. Addiction can, in many ways, feel chaotic and as though it has some power and control, but the way we transform our thinking to recognize our power makes all the difference. The best way to maintain sobriety long-term may no longer involve a "faith in something higher" approach or beginning our journey from a place of powerlessness.

For women, the idea of starting in a powerless position may even bring to light some negative associations with manipulation. Since society tends to arbitrarily define gender roles for us, girls and women are often expected to adopt a passive and amenable position. Sobriety requires us to speak up for ourselves, however, so that we can make our desires known to others, and so we can advocate for ourselves. In recovery, the saying "One drink is too many and a thousand drinks is not enough" drives home the point that sobriety only works long-term when a person views and accepts the idea that they cannot drink. While reducing the use of alcohol may help a person in the early stages of Alcohol Use Disorder (AUD), working toward a more permanent solution of long-term sobriety leads to more success in preventing relapses (National Institute on Alcohol Abuse and Alcoholism, 2021).

In the next two chapters, we'll look at alcohol's impact on our brain and how our mind can transform into a powerful tool for our sobriety.

Chapter 3:

The Powerless Mind

My reckless behavior in Manhattan in the 1970s was getting dangerously worse. There were some nights, even weeks when I decided I had too much of the partying lifestyle and wouldn't go out so that I could avoid blackouts. After some time, though, the urge to try again would return, and I thought I could head to a club and drink just a small amount and feel fine. This was never the case.

One evening in the fall of 1977, I headed to the movies with some friends and saw a film that would forever change my life and haunt my perception of myself. The movie was called *Looking for Mister Goodbar,* and it was about a young woman, played by Diane Keaton, who travels from bar-to-bar drinking, blacking out, then unintentionally waking up in a different man's apartment each time. One night, this woman heads home with a man who brutally attacks and murders her. This movie hit me hard, as I saw myself as this young girl in the film and now feared my tragic end if my current lifestyle didn't change. I'd like to say that this movie was the end of my drinking days and caused me to immediately become sober, but sadly, it did not. I did well in college; in fact, I was one of the top students in my class, but I was not smart enough to see that my drinking was headed in a terrible direction and needed to stop immediately. In my mind, I thought it would all work out somehow. I'm sorry to say that I also thought that getting married would give me the answer I needed. I figured if I could meet a guy I liked and marry him, I could feel safe because I'd have the same person to go home with each night. I know how ridiculous this sounds now, but in my 21-year-old mind, this plan made some sense. My drinking started to take over my mind, but it would still be years before I was drinking every single day. I'm sad to say that I got there eventually.

Power and the Brain

Even though the human brain is quite powerful, when we're under the influence of alcohol, it becomes fairly incompetent in language, decision-making, and motor functions. While drinking, we may feel like we have control over situations, movements, or brain activity when, almost all of the time, we don't have the control we believe we have. This can feel deceiving for those with Alcohol Use Disorder (AUD) since alcohol can make a person feel relaxed and briefly happy. Society has dubbed alcohol "liquid courage," but this feeling is fleeting and, in many cases, ends in regret. The sensation of relaxation and happiness is false, as this initial feeling quickly wears off and is virtually impossible to achieve again, leaving us feeling sad and upset that we can't maintain this feeling.

Short-Term Euphoria

For a brief period of time, drinking alcohol releases endorphins, like dopamine, that trick our brain into feeling elevated for a short amount of time (Editorial Staff, 2023). For many, once this feeling wears off, the brain sends the message that we need more alcohol to bring that euphoric feeling back, but this initial sensation of happiness we once had is challenging to recreate. Soon, we're chasing the euphoric feeling that we can never quite reach again but guzzling more alcohol to try to do so. This often leads to blacking out as a result of alcohol intake or is followed by overwhelming feelings of sadness or anxiety. This cycle is dangerous since the aftermath results in more and more drinking or leads to a "brain crash," which leaves us feeling empty and lethargic.

While the short-term result of drinking may feel like the relief we need to relax, this feeling is often confusing for those suffering from Alcohol Use Disorder (AUD). Is it the alcohol that we crave or the excitement we feel as we "enjoy" that first drink? When we start to consider why we drink, we may simply be craving the habit we think will bring us temporary happiness. While the short-term results of drinking include a sense of euphoria and reduced inhibitions, they also result in impaired judgment, loss of impulse control, and loss of memory. If you've ever awoken in the morning after a night of drinking feeling ashamed of the words you said or the activities you participated in the night before, you may have a close connection to this result.

Unfortunately, many people view the feelings of this short-term euphoria with a sense of power. After all, having power can feel like intoxication, and being drunk can often seem like a person has a sort of fake confidence. If we think that alcohol temporarily pauses some of the inhibitions and shyness, we may face every day; it's no wonder that people would constantly return to drinking over and over again to try to gain a feeling of confidence, even if this is never the actual result. This feeling is a temporary falsehood that makes us believe that we can be a better, more powerful version of ourselves while drinking. In society, we're taught that having power can lead to having more access to money and resources, so we tend to strive for this at all costs, even if it harms our health or friendships with others. Power won't automatically guarantee that a person is socially successful or develops positive networks with others, and while we think alcohol may help with this, it only provides a temporary chance to escape reality.

As children and teenagers, we're often warned of the dangers of succumbing to peer pressure, but as adults, we hypocritically end up following along with the crowd to strive for some connection with power and drinking. "Our human brains have mirror neural networks, meaning that similar brain areas are activated when observing the actions of others" (Azab, 2020, para. 7). If a person believes that another person is cool, confident, sophisticated, in control, or has any number of other appealing qualities, they often and subconsciously mirror this behavior without even being aware that they're doing so. In many cases, this is not a negative quality to have, as, at its foundation, it teaches us to feel empathy and connectedness with others. But when it comes to drinking alcohol or participating in other negative habitual practices, this mirroring clouds our personal judgment. Both men and women will react differently to viewing powerful role models, influential celebrities, or even friends they know differently, but if they view a person as someone they connect with and positively relate to, they may be more easily influenced by them in terms of the practices they engage in. For example, in advertising, is it random that companies often use well-liked, famous icons to sell products?

Choosing likable, popular celebrities to gain sales is a business in itself, and we fall for this type of marketing every day when we shop, whether we realize it or not. Once a person begins to recognize this aspect of society, they can also learn to avoid these noisy distractions since they often hold people back from making independent choices.

Long-Term Damage

Since we know that gaining that euphoric feeling from alcohol is a temporary sensation that requires more and more alcohol to achieve and never truly gets back to that original feeling, we can determine that alcohol will have many other long-term impacts as a person drink tries and gain that feeling once again. There are both physical and emotional impacts that drinking over time can cause. These include a much higher risk for liver damage, cancer, digestive problems, memory problems, and high blood pressure (Centers for Disease Control and Prevention, 2020). In addition, drinking can lead to negative social relationships with friends, family, and co-workers since it limits the control we have over our words and actions.

Over time, drinking can also have negative impacts on the brain, resulting in either a false sense of power or the opposite: powerlessness and desperation. If someone with impaired judgment feels powerful, even omnipotent, they might participate in dangerous activities that they normally wouldn't engage in while sober. This can later result in embarrassment, regret and ultimately damage confidence over time. Other people who are abusing alcohol might have feelings of desperation or powerlessness, which may place them at risk of suicide.

Alcohol also impacts the natural functions of the brain and results in a transformation and reduction of neurons that help send messages from one area of the brain to parts of the body (*Alcohol and the Brain: An Overview (NIAAA)*, 2022). In doing so, balance, memory, mood regulation, and speech control can be altered as a result. In many cases, blackouts become regular occurrences, causing periods of time lapses in the mind where a person simply cannot remember everything that happens while drinking.

This effect impacted me the most as I continued drinking in my teens and twenties. At first, I'd be aware of the night, then I'd blackout and not remember even half of what happened the next day. Part of becoming sober meant taking ownership over this aspect of my drinking, even if I couldn't remember every word I said or the action I took while blacking out. I knew I had probably embarrassed myself and others more than once while drinking and that I had work to do so that I could move forward from that period of my life as I began my sober journey. I had to talk myself into feeling power over this instead of allowing it to make me feel weak or sad about the moments in time that I couldn't remember. This realization helped me, and I believe it can help others, especially women, who are starting to become sober. Instead of feeling ashamed, anxious, or depressed about the events you wish you could have controlled while under the influence of alcohol, it's now time to appreciate the work you're doing to have more control and power over your current situation.

Modeling Power

Women, in particular, may feel they need to prove their worth to gain positions of power, so modeling the behavior of a close, confident friend or a woman in the business world may feel necessary, which can be positive until personal confidence is established. This kind of influence can also impact the way a woman attempts to gain sobriety and can actually work in her favor if she has a strong system. Seeing other women at sobriety meetings or hanging out with a group of sober friends can provide much encouragement for women seeking a non-drinking lifestyle, especially if a woman sees how positive sobriety can feel. Some of the most ambitious and optimistic women in my life are the ones who have maintained their long-term sobriety, and these women have guided me in my quest to continue to stay sober. When we hear the stories and experiences of other sober women, we can compare our similarities and differences but also enjoy the fact that we have arrived at a destination where we value our emotional and physical health.

In my time of maintaining my own sober power, I've had to make peace with many of the early parts of my life in which I made mistakes and couldn't understand soon enough how alcohol was affecting my world. If I had understood sooner, I would have, of course, made faster decisions about becoming sober earlier, but I've come to realize that, at any point in one's life, this incredible decision can be made and can be powerful. Whether you're sober-curious, meaning you're just starting to think about giving up drinking but may not consider yourself an alcoholic, or whether you fully recognize that you have an Alcohol Use Disorder (AUD), you're in the perfect place today to begin absorbing the positive long-term benefits that sobriety brings.

Chapter 4:

Transforming Old Habits

I graduated from college and worked in Manhattan in the late 1970s, but I still drank in clubs frequently. I knew I needed a change, but I didn't know what I wanted to do to alter my life. I was convinced that drinking wasn't negatively affecting me like it truly was since I was able to graduate and hold a steady job with no problem. I felt that this wasn't exactly what I was meant to be doing, and I was constantly searching for more excitement. I soon found it in ways that I could have never predicted.

About a year after my college graduation, I went on a trip with my best friend to Europe, where we planned to travel around from city to city in the summer using our Eurorail passes. We had just quit our jobs before taking this trip and were ready for any kind of adventure life was about to throw at us. I fully expected to visit and sightsee in Europe for a few months, then return to Manhattan, pick up where I left off, find a new job, and continue my life in New York. Instead, shortly after arriving in Spain, I met a guy who would change my world. I fell madly in love with him and quickly lost all sight of what my future in Manhattan would look like. Remember how I thought marrying a man would solve all my problems? Well, I married this Spanish near-stranger who would become my husband of 24 years. I barely spoke Spanish, but we had fun together, staying up late and drinking in the city. My friend met someone too, so we were both happy to remain in Spain instead of traveling around the rest of Europe. This felt like the new and exciting life I was looking for, and I wanted to dive quickly into it.

Spain, for me, was a magical escape where I thought I could do just about anything. I'd walk into bars in the morning and have a sandwich and beer while I people-watched. This life felt different from New York because it felt more exotic to me. I didn't want to leave and desired just about any change from my life in Manhattan. Did I mention I had a boyfriend back home? Oh yes, I'm not proud to say that I now had to choose between living a quieter, more familiar life in the United States with my boyfriend or trading this in for a new love and a new adventure. I chose the latter since this choice felt interesting and exhilarating.

We were happy for a brief six months before he hit me for the first time. I felt ashamed about it since I had gotten myself into this new life and wanted so badly for it to work out. My Catholic past was also haunting me, and I felt that I had to remain in this marriage at all costs instead of getting a divorce. Even if I wanted to divorce this man, strict governmental rules in Spain at the time prohibited this from happening, but I could have just walked away and gone back to the United States. Instead, I felt I was stuck in the marriage "for better or for worse," and I wasn't sure what to do. Little by little, I started to drink during the day. I felt out of control with everything else, so I figured, *why not? It's fine*, I thought; *have a drink, and everything will be okay*. Again, it never was. About a year and a half into our marriage, I learned some new information that would change my world again: I found out I was pregnant. I was very happy about that and stopped drinking. I thought the problem with alcohol was over for good, but that was not to be the case.

Clinging to Old Habits

While everyone has their own personal reasons for hanging onto the past, trying to grasp sobriety while continuing old habits rarely works. We might want to hold onto parts of our lives that provide us with comfort, familiarity, and predictability, but we often don't realize that this doesn't leave much room for growth and change. The harm here comes from the thought that we can continue functioning as if life is the same when, internally, we know that it will require work to produce the results we want. Compare this to a gym workout, for example. We know that if we want to get fitter, we need to put in the time and effort to stretch, complete cardio workouts, and lift weights, but if we don't create a habit of doing so, how successful will we be?

Women, specifically working women, and mothers, may find it especially difficult to alter their lives to create new habits or transform the old ones since many women tend to have a fairly structured routine. If you're a busy person, you may have moments here or there to squeeze activities into your day, but this often doesn't feel natural or normal. If a habit has been created, for instance, of always taking a coffee break at 10 a.m., then this ritual sticks with us, and we most likely start craving that break a few minutes before the event. The same goes for alcohol. If a person has developed the habit of drinking a glass of wine or two at dinnertime, it probably feels strange at first not to have this addition with a meal. We get stuck in a rut and don't know how to get out, but this is a feeling that many have fallen into, so we know we're not alone. Whether the habit is a positive one, like exercising or completing a daily chore, or a negative one, such as smoking cigarettes or drinking alcohol, people possess the ability to change habits; we may simply have trouble working up the desire to do so.

Habit Identification

For many, the setback to making a change in a habit starts with fear. *Why should I ask for that promotion when I know I won't get it? Why should I exercise when I know I'll never look fit? Why should I stop drinking since I know it relaxes me at the end of a long day?* Questions like these are inhibitions that drive our minds and force us to believe certain ideas that lead to false answers. Our brains want an excuse to believe them, so we say these negative words to ourselves. The fortunate news is that it only takes a short period of time to snap out of this mindset and start making real and positive changes. The hardest part though, is convincing ourselves that we need this change.

According to health officials, four aspects need to exist in a person's mind before they can proactively make a change (McPherson, 2022). These are:

- unhappiness with the current state.

- an idea of what the change would produce.

- action steps.

- innovative ways to achieve change.

When we boil down what's holding us back, what are we truly afraid of? If you're a person who doesn't consider yourself a fan of change, reflect on why this is so for just a moment. Even better, complete the following exercise: Grab a piece of scrap paper and draw a line down the middle of it. On the left side, write any goals that you currently have in life. These can be in any order and can range from small to large goals. Is there something you want to say to a loved one but are afraid to? Do you want to change jobs but feel stuck? Do you want to remain sober for the long-term? Write down anything and everything that may come to mind but try to write at least three goals on paper. This is just going to be for your eyes, so write down anything on this paper and know that you can tear it up and throw it out later. Now, on the right side of the page, line up each goal with one fear that comes to mind when you think of this goal. For example, if your goal is to stay sober, what fear holds you back from doing so? For me, I was afraid that I'd never be able to actually stop drinking. I didn't even give myself a chance, and for so long, I let this fear drive me to believe that I could never change.

Once you've aligned your fear with your goal, here comes the fun part. Start reframing the wording of the fear to create an affirmation for yourself. Add language to your fear statement that will serve as a small push to accomplish your goal. If, for example, you've written that your goal is to buy a new car within the next year, but you fear that you won't have enough money to do so, add some positive words to the fear column that could help you. This language could include, *I fear that I won't have enough money to buy a car within a year, but if I make coffee at home instead of buying a fancy coffee each morning, I'll have saved approximately $1,300 within a year. I can probably find other ways to save money throughout the week as well.* Yes, this does require a bit of creativity and talking yourself into completing the goal, but often that's what's needed to give a person that pushes to take action. If you have goals that just don't feel like you can add positive words to when reframing the fear, leave a space blank until you think about them a bit longer. Most actions are achievable, but they sometimes require thinking outside the box or talking the problem out with a friend to make some sense of how they can be accomplished.

If the idea of becoming sober is a fearful one for any reason, consider how you can push past the fear. Sometimes we're afraid to receive judgment from others when trying to become sober, which often takes a sense of power away from us. If we're living to impress others, we're not fully living, and some alterations need to happen. In his best-selling book *Atomic Habits*, author James Clear discusses the layers of behavior change. According to Clear (2012), we can focus on who we'd like to become and the habits we'd like to form or break by altering each layer. Layer one is all about changing our outcome. Similar to feeling concerned or fear over what we haven't accomplished yet, learning to first set the goal leads to the beginning of thinking about how we'll arrive at the outcome. The second layer asks a person to change their process. This entails actually taking the steps, or at least walking through the motions, to create or change a habit so that it will stick. For example, if your goal is to meditate for an hour each morning, waking up and immediately meditating for five minutes will help you create this habit.

While it may take time to work toward the goal of a one-hour meditation, simply starting at five minutes a morning trains your mind to start valuing this practice (Clear, 2012). The third and final layer involves changing identities. While this sounds scary, it's based on creating change for the betterment of our lives. If we've been trained to think that drinking is glamorous, for example, this can be altered by dissociation with the thought that this needs to be our identity. Instead, our identity could thrive on the idea that we're in control of our minds and powerful *because* we don't drink. It's not always easy to change the beliefs that we've grown up with, but change is possible when we rethink and reshape our identity to become what we want ourselves and others to see.

When a person fears that their identity may change if they stop drinking, this thought can pause the effort to become sober. Consider what may actually change, though. If you have a friend group that only meets to drink, would they be upset or make fun of you for drinking juice or water instead of alcohol when you hang out? If you think the answer may be *yes*, is this the kind of group you want to be around anyway? In most cases, we love the ritual of drinking, not necessarily the taste (Raypole, 2020). When we consider replacing the drink but keeping the ritual, we can still achieve the same goal for our brain. Even better, it can keep us clear-thinking and regret-free while still socializing with our friends.

Making a Plan

To gain control over any aspect of our lives, it's necessary to make a solid plan of action. Sobriety needs an action plan as well, even if it feels like there's only one goal in mind. If you're a frequent list-maker, writing a plan to track your sobriety goals may seem easy, but if this doesn't come naturally to you, it's time to practice. Creating daily, monthly, and even yearly habits and check-ins can spark momentum on a sober journey and help to have a set plan in place. While it's no use thinking too far into the future regarding sobriety, it is necessary to set goals that can get us to maintain sober actions. For example, starting a daily accountability check can make a positive difference in the way we start and end our day. Whether you're tracking your number of sober days using a phone app or simply writing a tally mark on a sheet of paper taped to your fridge, holding yourself accountable for each day of your journey provides some powerful insight into your progress. Even if there are lapses along the path of a sober journey, recording them on paper or electronically can help a person decide what patterns and impact sobriety is having on them.

When making a plan, take full ownership of your sober journey so that you can personalize the way you'll arrive there. Write down any triggers that you think may hold you back. Label any progress you make or struggles you push past as each day passes. Many people find that journaling their thoughts assists in making this sober process easier since they can attach notes to the times that are easy or difficult. If it helps, track how many hours you've earned each day by not drinking alcohol or write down an estimate of how much money you've saved by not buying alcohol each week. Over time, you can add up these numbers and feel even more powerful about the progress you've made.

As you personalize your plan, make a list of those individuals who will help you on your journey and those who may harm your sobriety plan.

When I first got sober, I knew that there were certain friends with whom I would now need to limit my time since our relationship was built around drinking. When I started thinking about my time spent with them, I even realized that drinking was the biggest thing we had in common and that we didn't have much else to connect us. They weren't ambitious people, and I knew spending more time drinking with them would only result in laziness for me. Start choosing people who will be on your "sober team" so that you'll know who to turn to when challenges arise. These are the people you'll talk to about your sober journey, and these are the friends who will support you.

Unfortunately, the friends you have who still drink may not be in a place to hear you talk about sobriety or the negative effects of alcohol, so instead of bombarding these people with alcohol facts, spend your time talking positively about your progress. These conversations can happen with anyone, sober or not, and making yourself a poster child for sober positivity can influence those around you without you even having to talk about alcohol at all. If Alcoholics Anonymous is a source of comfort for you, rely on these friends and sponsors in times when you need them. Groups like these are built to be a resource and community, so never hesitate to reach out to others who want to help. This is actually a sign of power on your part.

Just as AA and other groups may have a reward system when a person reaches a certain milestone of sobriety, create your own system of rewards for yourself. On paper or digitally, create a timeline of milestones so you can check in and reward yourself for completing this amazing work. While there's no requirement for how often rewards should be given, I'd suggest scheduling something special for yourself after each monthly milestone. The reward can be simple and doesn't need to cost anything unless you want to spend money on it. You could treat yourself to a walk in the park, some quiet time in the afternoon, or watch your favorite movie on the couch. Of course, you can get fancier with the rewards if you'd like, but the idea is to do something nice for yourself that will boost your motivation to continue staying sober.

Asking For Help (Yes, It's Okay!)

Do you hesitate to ask for help at work or at home because you fear that asking for it may make you appear weak to others? Asking for help is difficult but necessary, especially when we can't do something alone or feel we're in a dangerous situation. We need to rely on friends for support and guidance. Requiring assistance doesn't mean a person is powerless but rather inquisitive, confident, and powerful. It takes courage to ask for assistance with most problems, but when it comes to the sensitive subject of drinking, we need to show that we're powerful enough to recognize our vulnerabilities.

In many cases, our past experiences have shaped how we share or don't share our personalities and fragilities. When we hesitate to open up in front of others, it's often because we've felt shame or embarrassment about our previous situations as well. Our mindset for this new sober journey needs to alter if we're going to make any progress in this area. A key factor in staying sober long-term requires us to shut out the ideas we think we know and remain open to the opportunities we don't even realize are possible yet. If you feel your past still lingers over your ability to connect and share experiences with others, try practicing talking about your experiences aloud to yourself while driving to work, cooking a meal, or in the shower. Doing this exercise, even for a short period of time each day, gets us more comfortable talking about our feelings and with storytelling so that we can start to make connections with others.

Our most limiting beliefs often come from our minds, but this does not equate to powerlessness. According to the Steps Recovery Center, "our hopelessness, negative thought patterns, ways of thinking, and limiting beliefs fuel our patterns of mental illness and addiction" (*Why Is It so Hard for Us to Ask for Help?*, 2020, para. 8). In many cases, individuals can become upset or contemptuous in the early stages of their recovery. This feeling is normal because reflecting on the past while giving up a habit we've grown accustomed can feel difficult and often overwhelming at first. When seeking help with sobriety, know that showing vulnerability by sharing feelings with others can open a person up to making deep connections with others and doesn't need to be viewed as a sign of weakness. Becoming more vulnerable in certain situations may actually allow another person to reciprocate vulnerability as well. As humans, we love finding connections with others, so if we share a story or situation with others, we may just find that the other person wants to share with us as well, leading to closeness and camaraderie.

For me, having several powerful sober women in my circle of friends who I could talk about my sober successes and hardships was a necessity. I doubt I would have made it without these strong women to support and guide me. The strong women I've met understand the reasons for my sobriety, and they love the growth I've made along the way. If you don't currently have sober friends to help you on this journey, reach out to a sobriety support group to find people that have commonalities and can understand your personal story. This makes all the difference.

To more thoroughly explore the uniqueness of a sober journey in a woman's life, we'll need to examine some harsh realities of our modern society and discover ways to prevent certain situations from damaging and deterring us from our sober path.

Chapter 5:

Drinking and Sexual Assault

One of the more serious and long-lasting effects of alcohol is the trauma it can cause from a lack of coherency. Far too many women experience sexual assault as a result of this substance. Before flashing back to the story of my life in Spain and the news that would provide me with the biggest reason to get sober, my pregnancy, I want to take some time to reflect on the dangers that I faced, and that can easily arise while drinking so that other women gain even more awareness of its potential harm. Talking about sexual assault of any kind can trigger individuals in many ways, so if this information prompts difficult feelings, feel free to skip this section or read certain parts only based on the subheadings in this chapter. Know that the information found here can serve as a wake-up call for those who struggle with sobriety and can help navigate the world while newly sober, but if you believe this chapter will bring about too many difficult feelings at this time, you can revisit this section later as it will be here when you're ready to read it.

My Alcohol-Fueled Life

While in school in Manhattan, I kept my grades up, so many others didn't catch onto my Alcohol Use Disorder, even though I was drinking in public at least one or two nights a week. I worked, attended classes, saw my boyfriend on weekends, and kept up appearances as if I wasn't blacking out and waking up in a stranger's apartment often. Long before I had ever heard of the theory of being powerless over alcohol, I already was.

I started feeling terrible about my choices and lifestyle, but I didn't tell anyone for fear of judgment and ridicule. I had a Catholic upbringing, after all, and I was afraid those close to me would judge my morals, so

I hid many aspects of my lifestyle at this time. When I look back on some of my behaviors then, I'm shocked that I didn't end up in more trouble. The AIDS epidemic was about to erupt in the United States, and with my wild behavior, this very well could have impacted me if I had carried on with this lifestyle longer. When I got married and lived in Spain, I felt like that action at least paused the whole "sleeping at stranger's apartments" chapter of my life, but getting married didn't stop my drinking. I went from one terrible situation to another since I felt panicked and out of control in Manhattan and then married an abusive partner in Spain. In both cases, I wanted to stop the feelings I was having and the situation I was in, but I wasn't ready yet to face the fact that so many of my negative circumstances were a direct result of my alcohol abuse.

A "Fun" Night Out

Many women have experienced the scenario of going out for a Friday night at a bar or a party with friends. If we've had a long week at school or work, going out feels like an amazing escape from our mundane reality. If we're mothers and have hired a babysitter for an evening of fun, going out can also feel like a special treat that we need to make the most of because it rarely happen. Having a fun night out with friends gives us a great sense of release and, in some ways, power since we may feel a sense of saved-up confidence for nights like these, but this situation can turn dangerous when alcohol changes our senses and reaction time during these times.

When friends head out for a night of drinking, there are often many opportunities to interact with strangers they've never met before. These may seem like people that are comfortable to be around, especially when alcohol gives us an excuse to get closer to a person and say and do things with these strangers that we'd normally not do while sober. The question arises: How much trust can we place in a person while drinking? Even friends we have known for many years can become very different while under the influence of alcohol, so awareness of this is necessary. What's the best way to stay aware during a night out? Well, refraining from drinking is a start so that we can trust ourselves, our inner choices, and our power. Unfortunately, for a person with Alcohol Use Disorder, this is often easier said than done.

Assault and Alcohol

These two factors, alcohol, and assault, go hand-in-hand more often than they should, but this connection shouldn't be all that surprising since alcohol's influence alters cognitive and motor functions. According to researcher and author Mary P. Koss, one out of every three college-age women say that in high school or college, they've been a victim of sexual assault (Koss, 2022). In addition, about half of the incidents of sexual assault on college campuses involved the consumption of alcohol by one or both parties involved (The Maryland Collaborative, 2016). This is obviously a serious issue that certainly deserves more awareness and attention, but how can we highlight the impact of these statistics in a society that praises the culture of drinking?

While "alcohol should be seen as a risk factor for—not a cause of—unwanted sexual advances and other forms of sexual assault," it's important to consider how the public treats the perception of drinking (The Maryland Collaborative, 2016, para. 1). It's often a person's go-to method of relaxation after a long day, and we've come to see nothing strange with this perception. We often see movies or advertisements involving alcohol targeting younger viewers and creating the idea that drinking is sexy and expected of us when we enter high school or college. In many cases, simple parental advisory warnings for television shows or listing risk factors on labels are not enough to pause this behavior.

In considering the risk and damage that drinking can cause, "victims who were drinking at the time of a sexual assault report high levels of distress, self-blame, and negative reactions from others. They often fear they will not be believed or will be blamed" (The Maryland Collaborative, 2016, para. 4). While support exists for victims to help with the aftermath of the trauma caused by assault, women don't always feel comfortable coming forward to receive this aid.

Pressure and Power

Typically, when women go out for a night of drinking, many feel added pressure to drink more around their friends. If they try to choose not to drink, there's often a perceived negative and unnecessary stigma that goes along with this choice. On the one hand, not drinking can make a woman feel like an outcast, but on the other, drinking can lead to the ability of others to manipulate and control her.

Victims may feel that they could have done something differently if they had faced assault, and they may even experience guilty feelings, but this is not the reality that needs to exist. No abuse or sexual assault should ever take place, and victims are never at fault, even if this is not the way society always views this scenario. Abusers use power and manipulation to get their way, which leads to a false sense of trust for anyone, but women are more often the victims of this abuse.

The Impact of Assault

For women who have experienced sexual assault, there are often both short- and long-term physical effects as well as long-term health and psychological effects that result. The short-term physical effects include sexually transmitted infections, vaginal bleeding, unwanted pregnancies, or sleep disorders (Office of Women's Health, n.d.). Many long-term health issues are a result of stress and include chronic pain, heart problems, migraine headaches, sexual problems during sex, and digestive problems like stomach ulcers (Office of Women's Health, n.d.). Sexual assault also impacts the mental health of a person and can include anxiety, post-traumatic stress disorder (PTSD), and depression (Office of Women's Health, n.d.).

As a woman attempts to deal with the stress that comes from sexual assault, many turn to more alcohol and drugs to cope. While this temporary form of "dulling" the pain can make a person believe they're doing something to react to the problem, drugs, and alcohol can't provide a positive long-term solution. Because assault affects present and future relationships, including those with partners, friends, children, and parents, there needs to be a way for an individual to receive the problem's help to begin the healing process. The culture of drinking in social circumstances also needs to evolve for men and women to feel comfortable in public and private situations.

What Can Be Done?

In answering the question of what can be done to prevent sexual assault involving alcohol, more information and education are needed to address this problem. It sounds cliché, but information really is the most powerful preventative measure here. By educating young people about the dangers of drinking, especially teenage boys and young men, society can better prevent sexual assault from happening and can educate individuals about the negative results of alcohol instead of simply glorifying it. While changes to society's logic are almost impossible, bars and drinking establishments can start transforming their culture by establishing safer environments for all, especially women, who are more likely to fall under attack from sexual assault. In colleges, having more programs to educate all students about how alcohol and sexual assault circumstances are often connected can serve as a reminder to help reinforce the information for students.

If you or anyone you know has been the victim of sexual assault, the U.S. National Sexual Assault Hotline number is 800-656-HOPE (4673) (RAINN, 2000).

Predators in Unexpected Places

As someone who found AA helpful in many ways, I also recognize some dangers that can arise in groups like these. Specifically for women, the idea that's presented in AA of powerlessness can be problematic since this concept opens a person up to show their vulnerable side. This can sometimes be dangerous for a woman, who may be preyed upon or taken advantage of by others in groups like these simply because people see the opportunity to do so. An AA group that's strong can often see these predators and protect women from them, but this is an issue worth recognizing since it can impact the results of sobriety if and when it happens.

While this only scratches the surface of issues that can arise from alcohol and sexual assault, it's worth the warning if this is going to assist anyone in their quest to get and stay sober. Next, we'll look at the positivity that sobriety can bring, especially when establishing a powerful mindset from the start.

Chapter 6:

The Benefits of Power and Sobriety

When I discovered that I was going to be a mother, I knew I had to change. While this change happened quickly for me, it was a temporary one since I didn't yet have the skills to create a long-term sober solution for myself. Even though my situation was dire, I was thrilled to become a mother. I even stopped drinking for several years to have children and take care of them. I put my kids first, as becoming a mother was the most important event in my life. My marriage in Spain was still terrible, but I attributed this to my husband's late working hours and erratic behavior. Later, I learned that our money was not only going toward his drinking habit but also toward his diverse drug habits.

It was now the 1980s, and at this time in Spain, if a woman left her husband, she was viewed as abandoning her home or "abandono de hogar." If I took any action to protect myself and my children by leaving my marriage, I would automatically lose custody of my kids, even though my husband drank, used drugs, and was abusive. Yes, I was in a horrible situation at this time, and I didn't know how to help myself. As so many places were at this time, Spain was a country where women had very little legal power. Fortunately, legal rights for women in Spain have gotten better since the 1980s because of brave women who have spoken out regarding violence against women and girls in this country. During the period of my marriage, though, domestic violence was considered a "private problem," and if it was witnessed by others, it was something that they kept silent about.

A few years after the birth of my children, while I was no longer going out to bars or blacking out, I was still drinking at home and at work. I started drinking beer every day, and this began to feel like a self-medicating ritual for me. After having my children and eventually returning to work, I'd stash cans of beer in my large purse so that I could carry them around with me all day, just waiting for the opportunity to head to the bathroom to drink them. Each day, I promised myself that the next day would be different and that I would stop drinking, but the next day would arrive, and I would repeat my habit. By drinking several beers gradually spread out each day, I wasn't actually getting drunk, but I felt like I was reducing the emotional pain I felt about my lifestyle, even though this action was only making me feel worse each time. I was, without a doubt, addicted to alcohol and didn't want to admit it.

My logic during these days made no sense since I figured I'd be fine if I could just make it through the day by hiding my drinking while I continued to work and care for my kids. I was giving alcohol power, and I didn't know how to stop doing this.

Powerless to Alcohol

Have you ever taken a test that you felt completely unprepared for? Maybe you didn't study for it, or maybe you simply felt that the material was so difficult that you doubted whether you'd pass the test in the first place, causing a sense of defeat from the very start. When we feel that something is out of our control, we often give up before even trying. When taking a test, if we think or know we're unprepared for it, we're unlikely to score well. Alcohol also has this mental hold on a person. While people can feel powerless against alcohol, they can also be powerful people, but they may need to convince themselves of this fact before they can make any real changes.

In life, just as on a test, we need to feel prepared to face whatever's coming our way. While we don't always know what is ahead of us, having the skills to cope with stressors, the consequences of our actions and communication with others can help us achieve this power as we enter sobriety. While Step 1 of AA suggests that we need to feel powerless, I propose that this simply means that we can have a powerless feeling when it comes to alcohol but not be powerless people. In this chapter, you'll become more familiar with the benefits that the choice to become sober can bring so that the idea of staying powerful can remain in your mind as you step toward a better you.

The Obvious

In making decisions about sobriety, there are many factors to consider that will have an impact on an individual. Many studies point out the obvious benefits that sobriety has for the body, but there are also many benefits that sobriety has for the brain.

Brain Health

Our brains are incredible in what information they can hold and in how they can change or adapt depending on a situation. Even if we think we're turning our brains off for a bit to relax with a drink, we still store information and react to our environment, which can produce certain feelings in the mind. Before, during, and after drinking, the brain will expect an outcome that the act of drinking cannot actually produce, causing more dependency, depression, and stress. The more a person drinks, the more they become dependent on this behavior and expect it to result in a certain outcome, which rarely happens. Often, a person will drink more and more to try to stimulate a different outcome, but this kind of behavior only causes harm. Alcohol produces short-term dopamine, which makes a brain feel happy or "charged," but then is quickly followed by a drop in this feeling to levels that are below where the feeling initially began before taking a drink. This causes the desire to have a second or third drink so that the initial feeling can be recreated.

In studies of alcohol's effect on the brain, "alcohol produces chemical imbalances in specific neurocircuits and can be neurotoxic. Chronic heavy drinking can, for example, damage brain regions involved in memory, decision-making, impulse control, attention, sleep regulation, and other cognitive functions" (Koob & White, 2022, para. 2). While we've discussed ways that alcohol can impact a person in Chapter 5, it's important to understand here that the damage caused by drinking alcohol can also be reversed as a result of stopping this practice. More studies now show that, by becoming sober, lost brain functions can return and even have the ability to return fairly quickly once a person ends their drinking habit (*Brain Recovery after Alcohol Abuse | Life Works*, n.d.). Knowing this gives immediate power to an individual on their path to sobriety because it provides them with one of many reasons to start becoming sober. This also provides a great motivating factor for continuing long-term sobriety.

Body Health

In addition to regaining brain health, a non-drinker can see and feel daily benefits in their body. "Alcohol interferes with the immune system, preventing it from producing enough white blood cells to fend off germs and bacteria" (T, 2022, para. 7). When this happens, we're more prone to cancer risks, weight problems, skin problems, and general colds and sickness since we lower our immunities when drinking alcohol. Many feel improvements in their bodies after several weeks of sobriety since the toxins are released. Not only does alcohol deprive our system of certain essential nutrients to prevent sickness, but it also fills a person with sugar and useless calories that our bodies can't break down to produce anything positive for our system (T, 2022). Giving up this habit takes courage, but it also ultimately produces a naturally powerful feeling in the body since alcohol will no longer be taking hold of our system, leading to better overall health and clearer thinking.

The Not-So-Obvious

In addition to brain and body benefits, sobriety also provides some lesser-realized positive aspects to one's life. These benefits may take time to show results, but working with a support system of sober friends or family can bring out the power of these worthwhile advantages.

Relationships

While relationships can change and evolve after an individual becomes sober, a healthy relationship can become even better with sobriety. Those who show honesty and openness will thrive in their sober relationships, but even those who are not communicative can learn to reach out to others more since they may be focusing more clearly once sober. Open communication doesn't have to mean a person changes their personality from an introvert to an extrovert. Rather, it means that there's more of a willingness that exists, which can help a person share experiences, ask questions, and talk about problems to find solutions. Open communication can bring about positive conversations with others, causing relationships to grow and thrive. For a woman, having a sense of openness with others can lead to more opportunities for power in the workplace, at home, and in social circumstances since there's sometimes fear or intimidation that exists in groups with mixed dynamics. In romantic partnerships, having a stronger relationship with a loved one because the relationship isn't based on drinking or alcohol can lead to better honesty and improved conversations.

Self-Esteem

Recovery leads to healing, and when an individual feels whole again, self-esteem can flourish. Drinking alcohol causes a mood fluctuation that's difficult to control, but while sober, moods tend to be much more regulated. When this happens, a person can learn to store the tools they'll need to manage difficult feelings in future situations. Everything becomes a learning experience that a sober person can handle instead of an issue that causes them to spiral out of control. Sure, there will be challenges, but the ability to improve self-esteem because of the way a person feels while sober can motivate them to continue their long-term path.

Attitude and Positivity

When feelings are better regulated, we're likely to start living in unexpected and positive ways. Attitude improves, and a person can feel a stronger motivation to replace the addiction they once had with another more therapeutic or constructive activity. Sobriety is a personal journey and will look different for everyone, but feeling more energized to exercise, create art, change jobs, actively parent, or take a trip can help a person start living a more fulfilling life. Again, it may take time to reach a state where the energy increases, but with no alcohol in the body, we can start to feel like our best selves, so we become more productive.

Life

Our lives overall become more precious and liberating while sober. When a person feels health improvements, they can sleep better, make clearer financial decisions, spend prudent time with family members, find more confidence to try new things and improve work habits. While habits train us to follow the same patterns each day, creating routines that help us live in ways that we probably couldn't have imagined in the past is well worth the changes we can make in life to gain sobriety.

Working on Yourself

Many so-called "Quit-Lit" books will talk about embracing the idea that nothing is perfect during sobriety. There is, for sure, some truth in this idea, but by learning that you do have power over the decisions you make, even at the start of your sobriety, you can control the outcome each day. Everyone is a work-in-progress, especially when learning about sobriety and training their minds to become sober. This does not need to mean that we beat ourselves up if we slip or if we feel that we're still making mistakes along the way. It's important to stay honest and accountable during this delicate time, but it's also necessary to give ourselves the best self-care possible because we're healing and still tapping into our power. Making a mistake feels damaging, but it also leads to an awareness of what to improve on for the next round of life. Especially for women, taking ownership of the power we have to reflect on our progress each day and find moments of success when it feels like we've failed makes our journey that much richer.

It's time now to talk about creating lasting boundaries since this is often a difficult area to navigate for the newly sober. By creating boundaries that are needed, we tell ourselves and others that we're placing our most essential and present-day needs first so that we can prosper.

Chapter 7:

Creating Lasting Boundaries

When I first became sober, I learned that I would need to cut ties with certain aspects of my old life since I was now breaking negative habits and working toward a better life. Since much of my life revolved around drinking and the circumstances and people surrounding this activity, I realized this would need to change. This was more challenging than I thought since I was just learning about the boundaries, I would need to create between me, those who still drank, and my old drinking environments. I knew that if I was to succeed in long-term sobriety, I would need to develop new habits.

During this time, I did have several friends who drank regularly and whom I knew from drinking with them in social settings. Surely, I wasn't expected to just end all ties to any relationships I had while drinking? I consulted my AA group for advice on creating boundaries and heard some insightful and practical insight from those I trusted. They explained that personal boundaries were going to be important so that I could first discover what kind of person I could be while sober since I hadn't known this person for quite a long time. They also said that I should consider which people, objects, and actions were serving me daily and only focus on these for the time being so that this could help me achieve a new habit of self-care. These suggestions carried me and continue to inspire me.

What Are Boundaries?

Boundaries are not taught well to us when we're children. Young women, in particular, are often taught to act in a more passive yet nurturing manner, so we don't always learn to grow up with the realization that it's okay to break ties with others if necessary. From a young age, we're told to go along with an idea or activity, even if we don't always believe in it or want to believe in it. This type of submissiveness leads to confusion once we're adults since it's hard to decipher what a healthy relationship is and what it isn't.

While a boundary can look different depending on the individual, creating sober boundaries stems from a desire to be kinder and more loving to oneself by reserving time and energy for recovery. Setting a boundary may mean spending less time with others and placing priorities in different places so that a person can modify their lifestyle and care for themselves. This kind of self-care may also include creating a recognizable limit so that a person can have the power to make their own productive and sober decisions without the influence of others.

Your Needs First

It may sound selfish at first, but in recovery, the idea of placing your needs first is essential. This entails putting your desire to stay sober before other activities that may place you at risk or in danger. For example, a person may need to set more boundaries between themselves and friends who still drink. Saying "no" more frequently may also help to separate an uncertain and newly sober brain from the old habits in which it was once involved.

Think of your early sobriety as a period of healing. If you had the flu, would you run a marathon? While sobriety is not a sickness, you can still equate this metaphor with giving yourself the time to actually recover when it comes to taking care of your body and mind and learning the process of staying sober. This may also mean you need to simply be alone at times, or you need inspiration and to be surrounded by those who have not and will not influence you to drink.

When it comes to boundaries, there are several important types to consider so that your needs are established and met. These include emotional, physical, and time management boundaries (Bradford Health Services, 2023).

Emotional

Women may especially feel the weight of the connection with this type of boundary. In many cases, there is a need to set an emotional boundary because we won't have enough energy for other important tasks unless we recognize this need, but it's still difficult to create the boundary for this. We fall into a lifestyle rut and feel like we need to play a role in making people happy or keeping everyone at peace. This can take too much energy on our part, leaving no room for rest or mental clarity. Feeling like we have to keep going for others will often leave us feeling burned out and depressed about not having enough time for ourselves. Setting an emotional boundary means we recognize how much we can take on based on how much it will either energize us or drain us. If we feel we're taking on too many tasks that will deplete our energy or if we feel, in conversations with others, that our energy may feel drained, we need to back away from the situations we involve ourselves in so that we save the energy for ourselves and for the activities and people we love.

Physical

Placing physical limits and boundaries can be easy since this means dealing with the physical space of items and people, yet it can also be challenging since it can mean temporarily or permanently breaking ties with both of these. Communicating what physical space you will need is essential for this boundary to work. If you recognize that you need to remove all alcohol from your home, for example, telling loved ones this information can help them understand your need for others to respect this request and take this boundary seriously. If there are certain individuals that you need space from during this time, it may also be necessary to explain your need for this in a loving way so that your desire for sobriety is placed at the forefront of your life. In addition, if there are certain objects, like journals or motivational books, that you'll need to have around during this time but don't want others to touch or read, this request needs to be communicated so that the boundary is respected.

Time Management

Just as spending emotional energy on tasks can drain our minds, overscheduling ourselves can zap our ability to function. It's important to understand how involving ourselves in too many activities can catch up with us and make us feel exhausted. When addiction occurs, "people spend their time finding their drug of choice, using it, and hiding their abuse, and because of this, adjusting to more free time can be overwhelming for those in early recovery" (Bradford Health Services, 2023, para. 10). Creating a set schedule at first can help a sober individual manage the time they have available so they can reserve time for themselves and their priorities. While in recovery, it's helpful to have hobbies that will take the mind away from alcohol, but it's also necessary to not overcommit oneself so that there's still time to rest and relax.

Placing ourselves first during sobriety often means changing old habits and even modifying relationships that may not work for us anymore. Attending a support group or visiting a therapist is a high priority, and we should keep it that way. In doing this, we train our brains to recognize our needs so that we can more actively learn to highlight our own self-care for life.

Relationships and Communication

During sobriety, a person may feel that communicating a boundary to others means shutting people out completely, but this doesn't need to be the case. While we may need to limit time with those who at one point influenced us to drink, we can also be clear and straightforward with them about our expectations and what our new relationship with them may look like. "Setting boundaries is a way for people to be honest about their wants and needs in a relationship, increasing intimacy, closeness, authenticity, and satisfaction through mutual respect" (Nicole, 2019, para. 6). Whether we need to vocalize these boundaries to friends, family, or partners, doing so will honor our sobriety and help us show power in who we are during this time. Consider how you've felt when someone influenced you to do something you didn't want to do, and you simply did it to appease them. This never makes us feel powerful and usually ends in regret. By setting the boundary *before* you're influenced, you not only create the expectation that the limitation will be followed but also voice some accountability for yourself regarding the boundary. If your partner still drinks alcohol and you are working to maintain sobriety, for example, there needs to be a definitive expectation about what will happen when the two of you are together. Others may not always like that this boundary exists, but they need to recognize that it's there. If another person isn't giving you the space and respect you need at this time, then this is a red flag that you probably shouldn't be in contact with this person until you've healed more.

Break Ups and Forward Movement

Break ups are difficult, whether sober or not, and they can have a lasting effect regardless of age or situation. Realistically, there are times when relationships simply can't move forward, and people need to part ways. Sometimes this kind of separation may be needed temporarily, and in other cases, it may be needed long-term. If you've ever had to move on from a break up, you know what this challenge can feel like. If a break up occurs while simultaneously trying to maintain sobriety, this can create difficult but necessary outcomes. Staying sober allows you to feel all of your feelings, which at the same time can be both strenuous and wonderful. If and when you recognize that a parting of ways needs to take place to protect yourself and your sobriety, carving out time to reflect on your needs is one of the best ways to move forward. While a person shouldn't take on too many new hobbies during new sobriety, making time for activities to replace or distract from hard feelings can be a great way to continue personal growth and also stay away from drinking. These activities can be anything you want them to be since you're placing your needs first and feeling powerful while doing so. Sign up for an exercise class, take a walk once a week with a friend, or join a book club. You get to decide what will empower you!

Boundaries for Peace

When we don't speak up for ourselves or simply fall into a rut of living one monotonous day after the next, we can't find peace or power. To transform this habit and remain sober, we need to create opportunities for ourselves. If we're constantly pleasing others but forgetting our own needs, we're not showing ourselves that we own our power and life. By staying open to having new adventures, changing the way we've always thought about something, and creating new habits, we permit ourselves to take ownership of our sober path. As you get closer to creating the life you want, "a healthy boundary is paramount to maintaining peace within. When you restrict outside influences, you focus more on yourself. Reinventing yourself is necessary to live a life that you want to live" (Thalwal, 2022, para. 4).

You've heard the advice that can become your roadmap for a sober life, but let's now put these ideas into practice with adaptable ways to transfer them into your everyday life. In the next section, we'll examine how you can better tap into your power since it already exists in you but may simply need some assistance to bring it out.

Chapter 8:

Power Achievement Unlocked!

I've been figuratively "trapped" twice in my life. First through my alcohol addiction and then in my abusive marriage to a man in Spain. Even in 2004, when I finally decided to get divorced, I still felt trapped by the law since I was required to legally separate from my husband for two years before officially divorcing. This time was supposedly meant to give the two of us time to think about our decision before divorcing, but all I thought of was the abuse and danger that my marriage caused.

Unlocking my personal power took time, but I finally got to a place where I was ready to gain sobriety, freedom, and clarity. Deep down, I knew I had it in me, but alcohol was blurring this feeling and leaving messier results each day instead of the strength I craved. I had to unlock my power, so I quit drinking once and for all. This was the first and most important step that led me back to my power and eventually allowed me to recognize the freedom I could have in almost everything I took on. I could now begin making better choices so that I could support myself and my children. I could now be a responsible employee at my job and a better friend to others. I could build a stronger relationship with my parents and sister. Above all, I could put the energy I gained from sobriety into parenting my children effectively and lovingly.

Sobriety gave me a reason to start evolving more in my life as well. I started meeting the right people who would help me along the way. I stopped having relationships that were based around drinking alcohol and started finding meaningful connections with others. I even met the person who would become my partner for the next chapter of my life. I was waking up and feeling freedom for the first time in a long time, which brought me happiness that I want to share with anyone willing to take the next steps toward sobriety.

Get To Know Yourself

When a person starts noticing more about themselves, they gain knowledge of their likes and dislikes, which can help them stay on a positive track throughout life. When the ability to notice what we want or enjoy is dulled by alcohol, it's almost impossible to gain a sense of our true identity since we don't get to know ourselves on a deep level. One of the first and most important ways to exert power during a newly sober stage is to remember that you are driving your future and place yourself in a position of importance. You are the person who knows you best, but if you feel your life has been a blur for some time due to alcohol, then know that you can change all of this!

Start noticing what your triggers are, not only when it comes to drinking but also when it comes to any triggers leading to negative thoughts or behaviors that may be taking you down a dark road. Write down these triggers so that you're able to keep a working record of them and start becoming more aware of them. Triggers can come from many different sources, including physical and emotional stimuli. If you notice, for example, that feelings of boredom start to make you think about drinking, it's time to recognize this trigger so the feeling can be replaced with something else. For example, if going to a certain restaurant reminds you of having the alcoholic drink that you usually get at this place, it's best to avoid this restaurant for a while. By noticing what makes you feel happy, sad, angry, or frustrated throughout the day, you can begin dodging the negative triggers and filling your time with more satisfying activities. Having this awareness adds to the way we control our reactions, so we can feel more confident in the way we speak, act, and live.

If, in the past, you've allowed a relationship with a partner or friend to define you, it's time to say goodbye to this imbalance of power. This doesn't necessarily mean that you need to end this relationship completely, but you'll need to think carefully about what you're receiving from it. For example, if the answer mainly centers around relying on the other person to have fun and make all the decisions, then it's time to reclaim your power by spending some time apart. In this time away from the other person, figure out what it is that you want to do each day for entertainment and relaxation so that you can recognize your inner voice.

You've heard it before, but journaling your thoughts can truly help you understand what it is that you'd like to accomplish and explore in life. For a sober journey, deciding what is going well and what needs changing through the journaling process can become a perfect activity to gain clarity and motivation. In addition, deciding what goals are attainable or will be attainable someday can become a worthwhile topic to write about as one starts to understand what their new sober life will look like.

Becoming more mindful through meditation and yoga can not only feel therapeutic during this time but can also lead to more self-actualization. Setting a timer for even a small amount of time each day to sit and reflect or do some gentle stretching can incorporate a habit of mindfulness into the day, which will bring peace. Of course, there are also classes that a person could take to enjoy mindful practices with others, and these can help someone stay active, occupied, and social during their sobriety. Mindful activities can be simple and don't need to cost money to feel restorative. Simple and free activities such as watching a sunset or sunrise or relaxing with some soft music in the background can relieve stress and provide comfort.

Practicing a hobby or activity that you love or once loved can also give you a sense of healing and wellness. If cooking, dancing, painting, or gardening interest you, make a plan to add the activity to your weekly schedule so you have something to look forward to and so you can create a positive habit with this skill. Choose something you want to try and observe how this activity makes you feel while you do it. Not only will it give you a distraction, but it will also add to a feeling of completeness as you work on an activity you love.

Power and Support

As a person becomes sober, they can't underestimate the power of asking for help and obtaining support from others along the way. It may feel like an individual needs to get sober alone since this is a process that they ultimately control, but this rarely works, and it is necessary to have a support system in place that can give us more strength when we need it.

When asking for help at any time in life, use specifics. Try to clearly verbalize what the problem is and state what you will need. It's also alright to not know what you may need, but sharing the problem through clear communication can make a connection with another person so that they're aware of your need for support. Have realistic expectations of others if you'd like them to help solve a problem. They may not know how to begin with this either but give them time and ask if it would be reasonable to revisit this problem with them at another time once you've both had a chance to process it more carefully.

Professional Help

When becoming sober, it may be necessary to seek help from a professional counselor, therapist, or organized group such as AA so that others can assist with your sobriety. If you choose to seek support from professionals, it's especially important to seek support from professionals who are familiar with the process of sobriety and who have been trained to work with individuals in this area so that another person's impact can be as positive as possible.

By taking control of our own actions and seeking help from a professional, we can feel even more powerful for recognizing that this step is needed. Attending regular recovery sessions with a professional can provide a person with accountability, and while continuing the recovery process, this can become an important check-in for long-term sobriety.

Decide Who You Will Be

Gaining sobriety also brings a major benefit that many often overlook. This time can be a period to discover who you truly want to be now that you're newly sober. While no one can predict exactly what will happen to them in the future, a person can control their actions and words so that they can have a better chance of setting goals and creating the life they want. Take this time to think about what it is that will make you happy, what people you want to be involved in your life, and what actionable steps it would take to become the person you want to be. Journaling some ideas can help to create this plan, but you should also talk about goals with others that you trust so you can bounce ideas off them and hear feedback. Remember that you're ultimately in control and have the power to make real and positive changes at this time, but hearing ideas that others have may give you some direction for your sober life as well.

Writing Your Plan

As an exercise, try writing out the story of your life so far, flaws and all. Capture the major milestones and the highs and lows that you've experienced. Then write about this transitional time that sobriety has brought you so far. Decide what your life will look like moving forward. If you've always wanted to get a certain degree, change careers, or move to another country, write down these ideas and list what it would take to achieve them. Nothing needs to be set in stone here, as this plan is something that doesn't need to be completed today or maybe even ever. These are simply ideas on a sheet of paper that you now have that can be put into action if you choose to do something with them. Write down your plan for what you'd like to be doing five, ten, fifteen, and even twenty years from now, and brainstorm some ideas for how you'd get there. What small steps will you take today that can make changes to your future? We have more power than we realize to change our current state if something isn't working for us, so use this written plan as a reminder that there are accomplishments you'd like to make and that staying sober can help you achieve these plans.

Setting and Resetting Goals

This may sound a bit grim, but sobriety can often snap a person into thinking about their own mortality in a very real way. When we dull pain with substances like alcohol, we miss out on having real feelings and experiences that can help us set goals and consider how much time we have left. Once maintaining sobriety starts feeling easier, it's time to dream big with our bucket lists. This may be the first time in a long time that you've been able to consider what you actually want in life, so create changeable lists that you can adjust and adapt along the way as you learn and grow from sobriety. You have the power to make wonderful new chapters happen in your life; you just need to realize that you no longer need to be afraid of the feelings that alcohol used to dull. Even if you slip up along the way, you can restart your journey and set new and achievable goals. Consider what went wrong before and how you can start again to make the outcome better.

Starting small when setting goals helps us feel a sense of power over the outcomes and moments we control. Here's a helpful tip that my sponsor told me when I was newly sober: She said that if I find myself feeling anxious for any reason and am unable to do something therapeutic at that particular moment, like meditate, go for a walk, or take a bath, then the next best thing is to clean out my underwear or silverware drawer. Yes, you heard that right. These two drawers are usually not perfect, so they could use attention, plus they are manageable, fairly small drawers that won't feel overwhelming to organize. This was life-saving advice for me at the time since I had small children at home and couldn't often get out of the house or have time just for myself. I took her advice and used it during moments of stress. If you feel overwhelmed by setting major life goals, then try starting small by cleaning out just one drawer in your home today. By the time you finish, this activity will probably have taken your mind off the stress for a while, and you'll have at least one clean drawer in your house. Win, win.

Chapter 9:

A Woman's Guide to Values and Priorities

After my divorce, I was newly sober and cared for my children. I was still trying to manage my life in Spain, and with the way things were going at this time, I needed to take everything "one day at a time." While I was attending AA meetings and felt these were helping me, I was also struggling to find the time to create achievable goals since I felt like I was always caring for others around me. After all, this is my job as a mother, right? My days were spent working, running a household, and spending time with my kids. I was happy to do this, but I felt like I had no time to concentrate on figuring out the new personal values and priorities I'd need to create.

My needs, I imagined, were similar to many women's needs, but these were often pushed aside so that I could focus on satisfying others and making them happy. I needed to figure out how I was going to focus on my desires and what I needed now that I was sober, so I consulted trusted friends in my AA group to brainstorm some ideas. I had some years of sobriety, I felt strong as a person now, and I had the power to make good choices in most situations, but I also felt that if I was going to continue remaining sober long-term, I'd need to figure out how to balance necessary tasks while still reserving time for prioritizing my values and maintaining my identity.

As my friends and I thought about the best ways to navigate our lives now, we realized that we, as women, all had something in common. We were constantly searching for better ways to save time and energy for ourselves so that we could be more available for other people in our lives. This was a challenge for everyone I spoke with and was made worse by feelings of anxiety or stress. We had honest conversations about what would help us most so that we no longer felt obligated to carry the load of our household and could change the way society expected us to act. We realized that we needed to become a powerful force so that we could raise our kids and still save time for ourselves. Something had to change, so we created a list of our top priorities in life and discussed how we could value these while continuing to work on our responsibilities to our families and friends. While this was not an easy task, it gave us all some wisdom and insight for making tangible changes in our lives. This chapter covers these ideas as well as information about diverging from society's expectations so that a balance of priorities exists for you during sobriety.

The Old Ways

Historically, women have had to silently endure managing the lives of their families while trying to care for themselves as well. The unfair truth is that tasks are often completed, and schedules are managed without blinking an eye because women are the ones behind the scenes making the lists and carrying out the plans for many others. While this can sometimes feel burdensome, it has also become so ingrained in women to do this that many of us hardly question this kind of role as we juggle work, homes, and people in our lives. We often rush life so much that we forget to slow our pace and enjoy the situations that we're working so hard to create. This is the old way that needs to end if we're going to enjoy our sobriety.

If the last decade has taught us anything, it's that time is precious, and we need to make the most of it now. A person who is completing too much at once may not understand how to best prioritize their ideas so that these plans best meet their needs. Though Alcoholics Anonymous has existed for over eight decades, many of its core values haven't been updated for a growing and changing world. To combat this, we as women need to not only start standing up for ourselves in this alcohol-soaked society but also speak out against any antiquated attitudes that seem outdated in support groups. For a woman today, facing the challenge of getting sober can feel difficult since alcohol still has control over much advertising and pop culture. Completely reversing the way society feels about alcohol is unlikely without more public knowledge and people willing to highlight the negative aspects of drinking.

Since the 18th century, women have worked to make changes to social norms regarding sobriety. In the early 1900s, private meetings and protests were held that began conversations regarding the dangers of alcohol. Then, in 1969, a prominent action occurred that would help push this movement even further. "Marty Mann and actress Mercedes McCambridge spoke in hearings… before [a] Subcommittee on Alcohol and Narcotics. The hearings and these women's testimony resulted in new legislation and more awareness around addiction and the special needs of women with alcohol addiction" (duRivage-Jacobs, 2022, para. 15). In doing so, these women paved the way for more funding and research for the next generation.

While alcohol still plays a needlessly large role in everyday society, more women are now coming forward to speak about their experiences and to work on changing the way we think about alcohol. Sober bloggers and social media influencers provide more inspiration and comfort than ever before to the public so that a sober journey is normalized. While the future of any society is unknown, hope for more public awareness and interest in sobriety is possible.

There's a New Leader in Town

Though AA encourages anonymity on a public level, a woman doesn't need to be silent about her sober journey. By setting an example for others and modeling the practice of sobriety, a woman can start to be a powerful leader in her social circles. To do this, it's not even necessary to talk incessantly about sobriety. In fact, talking too much about the dangers of alcohol will almost always backfire on an individual. If the topic of your sobriety comes up naturally, others are likely to have questions about why you've made this decision. While it's fine to stay honest and straightforward with others about your sober journey, remember to stay mindful of the power you have in moments like this. You have the ability to give a quick alcohol-free sales pitch here, and others can take it or leave it. To do this, focus on talking about any positive changes you've felt as a result of sobriety. These could include the way you feel each morning, any improvements in your appearance or mood, or any increase in energy you feel overall. Try not to overwhelm another individual by being "preachy" or negative toward those who still drink. If the person you're talking to has ever thought of ending their drinking days, your gentle conversation may be just the push they need. For me, my friends and family know that I'm in recovery from alcoholism, or Alcohol Use Disorder (AUD), as it is presently known. One of the main reasons I've wanted to share my journey is to help break the stigma around alcoholism and the double stigma for women.

As a result of our typically strong ability to communicate well and manage many tasks, women make amazing leaders. Never underestimate your power during early sobriety, as you can find new opportunities for leadership at work, at home, and in social settings. It's likely that you'll find yourself feeling more powerful in your early days of sobriety since you've made a positive decision for yourself, so continue what you've started. If you already felt like a leader before becoming sober, you can now hone in on aspects of this feeling with greater depth and clarity. Don't let others tell you what should or shouldn't define you. With sobriety, you're going to understand more about your true personality and identity, so listen to that inner voice to start making powerful decisions for yourself.

Forget What You Know

When considering the power you'll receive from sobriety, it may be necessary to keep the past in the past and start fresh with this journey. While aspects of our past shape us and provide us with teachable moments, our ability to start over by becoming sober gives us a chance at a new life. Erase the woman you think you need to be and start enjoying this journey. Think of every positive aspect of what sobriety can bring for you. Even better, write this list in a journal and revisit it when you're feeling overwhelmed or anxious.

If you start questioning your own power or leadership, remind yourself of the path you're on and how you can change the course of the future, not only for yourself but also for others. You can be a leader in many aspects of your life, from work to parenting. For a woman, "becoming a leader involves much more than being put in a leadership role, acquiring new skills, and adapting one's style to the requirements of that role. It involves a fundamental identity shift" (Ibarra et al., 2013, para. 2). Many women have been told for so long that they can't do certain things in life that it's hard to reset their minds to think differently. By shifting our approach to thinking we *can* do something, we alter our identity and, often, the outcome. Forget what you've been told and start living as if you haven't been told "no" before. Create a positive role model for others and seek opportunities that will showcase your abilities.

Prioritizing Your Sobriety

When I became sober, I had a difficult time understanding how to place my sobriety at the forefront of everything I did. It felt as if trying to stay sober would take over my life and leave me feeling exhausted since I wasn't used to it. Sooner than I expected, I adjusted and learned to stay in control of my life since I was saving time and learning more about the person I wanted to be. I started feeling like staying sober was easy if I just listened to my inner voice. I replaced the feeling of wanting a drink with, well, whatever the hell else I wanted to do that would feel positive and therapeutic for my journey. I started to write more, attend group meetings for support, spend energized moments with my children, and fall in love with my life. I was able to stay powerful by prioritizing responsibilities, remaining calm in stressful times, and solving problems when needed. My brain became sharper, and this made me feel the pure confidence I needed to excel.

When a person doesn't feel in control of their life, it's hard to make any decisions about moving forward. One of the most surprising aspects of gaining my long-term sobriety was how little I thought of alcohol once it was flushed from my system and once, I realized how little it had done for me in the past other than cause damage. I not only felt "normal" again but felt elevated like I could start taking on new projects and plans that I had always been meaning to accomplish. Sobriety became easier each day since I never wanted to feel lost or out of control with alcohol again. Any stigma or shame that ever arises in conversations about sobriety usually comes from those who aren't sober and don't understand its power and benefits. It's time to change any public perception of negativity associated with sobriety by showing others the example that you, as a leader, can set.

While sobriety is a very personal experience for everyone, several methods of action can help a person when difficulties arise. In the next chapter, we'll examine ways to receive even more power in your life so that you can take charge of each day and feel composed while doing so.

Chapter 10:

Actionable Power

My biggest wins in life have happened within the last 33 years of my sobriety. Does this seem strange to me? Not at all now that I know what capabilities I have. At this point in my life, it's hard sometimes to remember what it felt like to feel powerless or out of control. I've made a fantastic life for myself and my family in Spain. Since I've lived here for over 40 years, when I consider the hardships, I faced when first arrived, it feels like a distant memory. Throughout my life, I've been a student, nurse, teacher, and, most importantly, a mother and grandmother. Each new adventure for me has felt attainable since gaining my sobriety so long ago, and I continue to make plans for myself that I know I have the power to put into action.

My ability to live a healthy and happy sober life comes from my desire to continue self-improving each day. Staying sober long-term has given me the power to contemplate and make important decisions. It's given me the motivation to travel and write so that I can share my stories with others. At the forefront, it's given me the power to be free.

It's Time for Something New

Sobriety comes with challenges, and each day needs to become a do-over for anyone working to stay sober. Consider what old ideas may have held you back and what you may need to change so you can grow. This may include making difficult decisions regarding old friendships and places you once visited, but the outcome is well worth this change. If you used to drink in bars or at friends' houses, try to pause visiting these places so that you can replace these activities with new ones that bring you positivity and progress. Involving yourself in new sober activities and spending time in new sober locations can help bring about a sense of inner worth and happiness for your "new life."

When you decide which people will comprise your "army of amazingness" during your sobriety, invite them to take walks, join a class, or just chat over coffee with you. Having friends that are encouraging and will support your sobriety instead of coaxing you back in a dangerous direction will add to your strength. These don't necessarily need to be friends who are sober, but they do need to be aware of your commitment to sobriety so they can support you in staying sober.

For women, finding an outlet for fun can be difficult when life gets busy, but looking for ways to start a new project or hobby is one of the best ways to stay focused on a task during a newly sober stage of life. Choose a mild activity that isn't frustrating but that you can do when you need a break from the world. While staying motivated, this activity should help calm and relax your system. Even completing chores or organizing around the house can become somewhat therapeutic during the recovery process. Change is often hard, but finding ways to move forward and feel powerful will make a difference in successful sobriety.

Calming the Mind

A mind that's trying to cope with the busyness of each day is not going to be as productive as it should be. In addition to yoga and meditation, there are other quick, simple ways to calm the mind that can quickly bring a person back to the reality that they don't need alcohol and are doing something amazing for their body by staying sober.

First and foremost, limiting social media during a time of new sobriety can bring peace to a chaotic mind. Seeing what others are doing, saying, or drinking in pictures and with captions on social media can lead to the feeling that you're missing out when, in fact, these types of social media updates are just a false reality of what's really happening. Social media can often make us feel powerless because it gives us the sense that we're not doing enough, but by limiting or eliminating social media during our new sobriety, we won't become absorbed in that world that can make us feel inadequate. This can allow us to tap into even more of a sense of power during this time since we'll receive time back for other activities by not checking or creating posts on social media. Let this time be just for you.

Finding time for yourself each day leads to more opportunities for clearing the mind and caring for ourselves. Sitting and relaxing for just a few minutes daily can have a large impact on the way we carry ourselves throughout the rest of our day. Even simple, necessary tasks like taking an uninterrupted shower or bath, or washing the dishes after a meal can allow a person to think and calm their mind since, with activities like these, we often find ourselves on autopilot and can simply "zone out" for just a bit while we complete the task.

Exercise is another way to achieve a sense of calm, even though it may sound like it would do the opposite. When we exercise, we release endorphins, which increase our overall happiness. Even if, at the moment, we think we hate exercising, the benefits of getting a workout can stay with us long after we end the activity. With exercise, our brain may be learning something new, such as the steps to a dance, or it may be calming itself to settle into a repetitive workout, such as walking or running. Either way, this kind of "work" for our bodies and minds helps stabilize our systems and provide them with increased energy for the long-term.

You've heard it before, but getting enough sleep at night helps the body and brain recharge and recover from each day, so you can be your best self when you wake up in the morning. By turning off any electronics and getting ourselves to bed at a consistent time each night, we give ourselves a head start for the next day and journey. Naturally, without alcohol in the system, our bodies will also feel the benefits of waking up refreshed rather than hungover. Many of us are often trying to chase a perfect night's sleep, and during the first months of sobriety, this can be hard. As our nervous system heals with sobriety and we have a chance to try a few calming practices before bed, this goal is possible.

Learn From the Past

When we reflect on the past, we learn about the future. Often, mindful activities can assist with reflecting on previous endeavors, mistakes, and conversations so we can receive insight into what may be needed in the future. A sober person can take comfort in the fact that the conversations they're now having with others are clearer and more concise instead of messy and embarrassing. Never feel that you need to dwell on the past when it comes to previous mistakes or conversations, as long as you're taking action to ensure that progress is being made in your life. By staying sober, you're showing that you have the power and knowledge to improve your future. You can reflect on any so-called "failure" from the past, then use it to direct your future, improved actions.

Since it can be difficult to think about missteps or conversations we had in the past, especially while drinking, it may be necessary to start small and make new improvements. Consider any subtle advances you can make as you strive for growth. The idea isn't to become perfect but to respect the process of self-improvement so you're then able to have better conversations with others, clearer decision-making abilities, and stronger self-esteem. Say goodbye to feeling like what you've said or done in the past was a mistake and, instead, view it as another chance to learn.

Take Your Time

One of the most important pieces of advice I received when I first got sober was to not try to rush to the end of my journey. So frequently, we don't have the chance we need to slow down in life and simply take our time to live, but sobriety can force us to carve out new times for ourselves in the best way possible. Since sobriety is a lifelong process, you don't need to feel like you're in a race to an end result. Instead, use this as a chance to start learning *how* to live in this new and improved way. Take more time to enjoy meals by sitting and eating slowly. Stay mindful of the sights, sounds, and smells around you. It sounds corny but soak up every aspect of life because we only get one, and sobriety is similar to being reborn. Don't take this gift of newness for granted.

You now have the chance to live like a child who is fascinated by everything around them because you can now feel, see, touch, smell, and taste with a new clarity that provides lucidity.

Society's unkind expectation for women is that we'll be the carriers of tasks, even if these are burdensome. Many women begin feeling like martyrs as a result, but this no longer needs to be a woman's outlook once they're sober. Yes, women have the ability to manage many tasks in life, but they also possess amazing intuition that helps guide them forward in decision-making. By listening to what our body and mind are really telling us while sober, we can continue to be more creative, loving, and hopeful for every upcoming task.

Chapter 11:

Setbacks and Restarts

During my first year of sobriety, there were major roadblocks that made me want to quit my journey. I almost did several times, but I had the comfort and compassion of sober and strong women in my circle of friends who helped me through my darkest moments. One myth of the sober journey is that a person will first be required to hit "rock bottom" before becoming sober (MacFarlane, 2021). While some people have a pivotal moment that makes them realize they need to become sober, many others simply do so because they've discovered that, after getting over that initial period, which is often hard, the way they feel without alcohol is extraordinarily better than with it. Setbacks and slip-ups may happen, but this doesn't mean that a restart is impossible; it simply means a person has more to learn.

If you've felt the difficulty of temptations or setbacks during sobriety, it's important not to let this hold you back from trying again. While having to restart your sober journey from Day 1 again will feel frustrating, think about your learning process. Is it with ease and perfection the first time you make an effort to try? In most cases, excellence isn't easy and doesn't come immediately. It takes time and effort to improve upon anything great, and becoming sober is one of the best things a person can do for themselves. As we say in AA, it is progress, not perfection, that we aim for.

Any individual wanting to gain sobriety has a chance for growth and change, regardless of their past. If a slip-up with drinking does happen, this can feel like a terrible catastrophe since a person may think they've undone all of their hard work. Instead of dwelling on this moment, use it to gain power and push past this setback to start again.

At first, I was overwhelmed by the idea of my sobriety being "forever." *You mean I'll never have a drink again? Like, ever?* My newly sober friends would often talk about this feeling too, but many of the individuals who had stayed sober for years gently told us that we were thinking of this idea all wrong and that there was a better and more healing way to consider our sobriety. While, yes, the idea is to stay sober long-term, this isn't a productive mindset to have at first. To start, a newly sober person needs to think of sobriety in small, bite-sized pieces, focusing only on small chunks of time before moving through the hours, days, and then eventually the weeks, months, and years of sobriety. Taking this time as it comes and remaining open to the fact that this is a learning process can keep a person on track for the long haul. My friends and I listened, but we didn't really understand this until we experienced sobriety for longer. Eventually, we started talking about the fact that we had been coming to these meetings for several months and didn't even realize so much time had passed. Life wasn't boring or repetitive like we thought it would be since we were finding new ways to listen to ourselves and do what we wanted to do. We found power in every new thing we tried, and the thought of drinking diminished each day. Our days turned into weeks, then months, and finally years.

A Goal Reminder

If the thought of having to undo any hard work you've put into sobriety makes you nervous, it's possible to curtail this with a simple activity you can start to complete today. Revisit that sheet of paper where you wrote your original goals so you can receive a quick and urgent reminder of why you want to obtain sobriety in the first place. Remember back in Chapter 4 when you were encouraged to make a plan by sharing goals that you wanted to make achievable as a result of your sobriety? If you have never made this list, it's not too late to start, as this can give you the fuel you need to either start the journey or continue it in a healing way. By consulting your original sobriety goals, you remind yourself of the people in your life that you want to feel closer to or the activities you still want to accomplish.

Hold yourself accountable for the goals you create by reading your list of goals to a trusted partner, friend, family member, or sponsor. This person should have similar sobriety goals to you, but your ability to trust this individual is what's key. Find a friend with a great ability to listen and read your goals aloud to this person, plus share how this individual can help you reach them. The suggestion may be as simple as reminding you of these goals every once in a while, if that's what you feel you'll need to stay on track. In addition, you should regularly revisit your goals to remind yourself of what this journey means to you, so keep this list in a convenient location or even carry it with you throughout your day. Allow this list to serve as your motivational paper when you're out in public or starting to have any negative feelings and need refocusing.

While saying an affirmation to yourself can sound silly, doing this one act each day has some real power. By repeating affirmations like "I can do this" or "I am powerful" five times aloud every day, you tell your mind to start accepting this idea, even if you feel you don't believe these words at first (Simmons, n.d.). Imagine you're talking to your best friend if that helps. What would you say to this person to help them push past their doubt, fear, or anxiety? It is important to actually say the words aloud to hear yourself showing power and courage, so don't skip this action. More than likely, you'll find yourself starting to speak and think more enjoyable statements about yourself over time.

In the beginning stages of sobriety, create a set daily and weekly schedule for yourself. This will help curb any temptations to go out with friends who may negatively influence you and throw you off track with your goals. If you want, purchase a special calendar or day planner to use just for your sobriety goals. Doing this also helps to hold you accountable by knowing that you've gone out of your way to purchase this calendar and create a special agenda for yourself. Try not to become upset if not everything you're setting out to do gets accomplished. Remember, start small so you can build power and momentum over time. Simply having a physical plan on paper will give you something to look at and strive for, so you can stay on track each day and feel proud of your accomplishments.

A person will only be able to feel power if they feel they're able to control their path, even when it's hard to redirect choices and change decisions. Taking ownership of the way we determine ideas takes courage, but this is courage that you already possess. Remember that your goals can help bring forth the confidence you need to stay strong each day.

Love Yourself

By seeking some enjoyment from the activities we're participating in each day, we make room in our lives for practices that show love and encouragement for ourselves. Finding time to rest is always important for self-care, but so is giving ourselves new chances to grow and explore. If you don't feel comfortable engaging in an activity or feel like another person is holding you back from achieving something you want to do, give yourself the space and time to be alone with your thoughts. Separate yourself from anyone who doesn't make you feel loved or supported. In doing so, you give yourself the ultimate gift of composure and adoration.

Start speaking more positively *about* yourself. When we start believing the affirmations we tell ourselves, this gives us a chance to spread our confidence and positive self-talk to others as well. This doesn't mean that we brag about ourselves to others; we simply take the time to say "thank you" more often when we receive compliments instead of finding flaws to explain away the accolade. This also means we self-reflect in a more positive and healthy way since this will eliminate the self-deprecating words that seep into our system without us even realizing it. If you find your head insulting or criticizing yourself, stop and restart your thoughts with positive words. This will take time and a lot of practice because you have probably developed a well-traveled path in your brain with years of negative self-talk. Remember to talk nicely to yourself, and if you aren't doing so, tell yourself to stop and bring your thoughts to a new path.

Finally, stick with completing the activities that make you smile right now in life. You'll be able to take on so much more in the future, but finding activities that relax and ground you right now will help you create a positive and protective boundary for your sobriety. These will become the powerful go-to activities that can help you before a relapse occurs. If you happen to need a reset, these activities can be the ones you choose so you can pull away from any self-doubt and fear to get back on track. By loving ourselves even during slip-ups, we acknowledge that we're not perfect and use this chance to refine our power so we can try again.

Helpful Emergency Support

Make a list of your top three trusted people that you know you can personally rely on in life when times are hard. Go on, try it. Do this on a sheet of paper with your goals if you'd like, or write their names in a journal. These people can be family or friends, but these are going to be the ones you can call on if or when you feel like you're tempted to stray from sobriety, so it's helpful if they are also non-drinkers and understand the feelings you may be having. These people don't need to know each other but give each person the message that they're your go-to people in times of emergencies. Explain your reasoning for choosing them as well, since this is likely to not only flatter them but also give them a personal sense of accountability to help you.

In that planner or calendar you're keeping, schedule a check-in with one or all of these individuals at least once a week so you can touch base with them about any challenges or triumphs. This doesn't need to be a long conversation unless you want it to be, and you can even weave this weekly report into a walk outdoors, a friendly phone call, or brunch together. The idea is to gauge your feelings by communicating with another person so you can see what could help you continue completing your steps in sobriety. Even a short ten to twenty minutes of reflection can help hold you accountable for your actionable goals.

You may find that it's necessary to receive more professional help to discuss your sobriety, which is perfectly fine as well. If this is the case, seek help from a counselor, therapist, or doctor specializing in sobriety. Talking to one of these individuals is a great way to increase your power since you'll become more aware of the strategies and suggestions they may offer each time you speak with them. In any week of new sobriety, it's fundamental to consult your bank of resources, which are the people and activities that are going to make you feel confident and powerful. If a person or action is making you feel the opposite, try consulting something or someone new to gain the benefits you need.

Keep Moving Forward

One of the hardest feelings in life is the feeling of defeat. World-class athletes, major companies, and celebrities all face this, however, and many push past it by considering how they can make any changes for the next time. While this isn't easy, "there's a big difference between lingering on a failure and taking the time to accept it, process it, and glean lessons from it" (Boitnott, 2014, para. 3). If you have to restart anything in life, especially your sober journey, see this as an opportunity to simply begin again. Think of it as no more than that. Starting again doesn't have to deplete your time and energy since you know even more about what you'll need to do to succeed next time. Regardless of past failures or moments where you were made to feel powerless, you have the ability to go from one action to the next with grace and poise.

It's also time to find some active positivity in the way you conduct any changes in your life. Besides taking chances on new activities to replace any negative habits you once indulged in, find time to take breaks, rest, and feel okay with being by yourself. Surrounding yourself with people who bring out the best in you while sober is wonderful, but you'll most likely feel even more power when you realize you can rely on yourself for fun and entertainment, even in uncertain times. Start to realize that you have the power to create the change you want in your life and that you're in control of these adjustments.

Finally, take new and positive risks! Now is the time to try a new activity, hang out with a newly sober friend, or start working on a task you've been meaning to do. If you keep yourself constructively busy and have a task that you look forward to each day, you're likely to find that sobriety becomes much easier and more lasting.

Since you're learning to come a long way with your personal sobriety, in the final parts of this book, we'll focus on how you can use this newfound energy to bring positivity to others and fully enjoy the connections you can make through staying sober and powerful.

Chapter 12:

Maintaining and Sharing Power With Women Everywhere

Despite all of the disastrous behavior, challenges, and setbacks I've faced in my life, I'm in the best place possible at this moment. I've realized that I'm enough and that I can be perfectly happy living in the present. If you had asked me in my 20s what kind of life I'd want for myself, I would have told you that I saw myself staying in Manhattan, holding onto my job, and eventually marrying and having a family. My path meandered, but would I change any of my experiences to get here? Nope. The lessons I've learned, even from my setbacks, led to the positive experiences I've had in finding my power and authority. I tweaked and reframed my goals so that they would work best for me, and I now have an amazing life that I can share with the people I love.

I'm still living in Spain but am now retired. I've been married to a wonderful man for the last 19 years, and I have three grown children who are all successful. It makes me tear up just thinking of how proud I am of them. They have children of their own, who I get to see often, which is a reality that probably wouldn't have happened had I not been sober for all of these years.

My mission in life is to support myself by uncovering my inner power each day but also to use my power to support other women who face challenges and need help with sobriety. I still attend an AA support group in my local town. Here, I work directly with women, especially newcomers, to help them realize their power and potential with sobriety. Just like all those women were there for me years ago, I dedicate my time now to working with sober individuals to offer them support, advice, or just a kind ear.

Women Unite!

Building mental strength and fortitude is something we could all improve upon. When I was drinking, I felt the pain of feeling like I had to compete against other women, but this might have just been my distortion of reality due to my low self-esteem. Since I became sober, I have only wanted to join forces with women to build them up. It's time to change this convention once and for all. When we share experiences, tips, and successes with other sober women, we invest in a woman's power for the future. As women, we have more power than we realize to start making societal changes today, just as women before us did when they rebelled against traditional ways. To do this, we have to start viewing other women as inspirational and celebrate the influence we can have on society.

If there's anything that I've learned over the years, it's that we don't need to be walking alone on our sober path; instead, we can be a tribe leading each other to the same sober destination. I want to see us cheering for each other's achievements along the way so we can honor shared success instead of competing for it. This is the way women become stronger and even more influential across the globe.

Power Over Yourself

Hopefully, by now, you've realized that your power comes from within and that, with each passing day, you're getting stronger. It doesn't matter how young, rich, or lucky you are in life; sobriety can be an equalizer for all of us, but one where we can share its benefits instead of struggling each day just to survive. When people realize they have no one to impress but themselves, they can start to live a much fuller life without the desire to drink simply because others do or because they think it will help them relax. Alcohol only creates more chaos.

No other person should have power over you, and if it feels as though they do, a change needs to take place. Finding opportunities to be yourself by feeling comfortable on your own can lead to a better understanding of your personal needs and desires. Spending time on your own leads to feelings of power and the acknowledgment that you don't need to rely on another person to live. Sure, you probably have people you love in your life, but never underestimate the power you have within yourself to enjoy your own company and the person you are. While organizations like AA offer a sense of community, which is valuable and important, know that you can make decisions and rely on yourself for joy each day while appreciating the person you are. If you let someone else control this, you're denying yourself the ability to know who you are. One of the best ways to gain long-term sobriety is by getting comfortable with little daily progress and teaching yourself what's important.

Power Outside of the Home

As women, we need to view and recognize the value of other sober women in our lives. If you currently don't know other sober women, take some time to create some friendships, as this can be life-changing! The most influential and ambitious people I know are my sober friends, who are women. I'm constantly in awe of them and appreciate the way they make each day look easy and effortless, even though I know it isn't always this way for them. In my case, I found my friends through AA, but if you don't belong to a group like this, think of women in your life who don't drink and who you could get to know better. If this feels difficult, try joining an online group of sober women or attending a meeting in your area for sober groups to meet new people who can support you.

By joining forces as a community, sober women can become role models for each other and for anyone who is not yet sober but may want to be. Being a role model for others also empowers children, teenagers, and young adults to celebrate a new standard of living. Drinking doesn't have to be the norm, and sober groups have the power to spread this message through the example they set. In public settings, drinking alcohol doesn't need to feel like a requirement for fun. Individuals who don't drink should never feel like outsiders since this practice sets a better example for others. Being able to stay engaged in conversations, listen actively, and remember meaningful exchanges is a positive way to socialize, and sobriety can bring this to each of us. Showing others that it's no big deal to remain sober is also an eye-opening model for them. Many drinkers seem shocked by hearing that someone is sober, but to engage in a long, drawn-out response to this kind of revelation only makes sobriety more mysterious to others. The only real response needed is to maintain your composure, energy, and fun. We can demonstrate to others that sobriety doesn't need to feel like such a difficult change in life, which will set the best example for others.

In the workplace, women who have confidence often start gaining more leadership roles and responsibilities. This kind of attitude doesn't come without fear or insecurity for all of us, though. "Failing well takes courage, but it is also something you can get better at. Volunteer for a project or task at work that makes you nervous (but doesn't terrify you)" (Simmons, n.d., para. 20). Sobriety assists in all walks of life, but especially in trying to get ahead with a new feeling of renewal or confidence. Spreading this feeling helps shift society's thinking so that it's natural and expected for women to be in positions of power.

Maximize Your Sobriety

To personalize this journey for yourself even more, seek ways to better understand yourself and those around you. While sobriety will be an extremely individual experience, it will also be one where you'll need to incorporate the considerations and cues of other sober individuals who can help you. "There are many paths to recovery. People will choose their pathway based on their cultural values, their socioeconomic status, their psychological and behavioral needs, and the nature of their substance use disorder" (Substance Abuse and Mental Health Services Administration, 2016, para. 5). Anyone seeking sobriety needs to acquire time to realize their potential and value, since grasping this may be a new concept. There are times when being alone on certain days can help you process your thoughts, and there are other times when surrounding yourself with people will give you the most energy, strength, and power. This is a personal preference, so don't feel lost if you want to be alone during certain stages of sobriety. If you do start feeling powerless during recovery, it's time to seek assistance from a support group, therapist, or doctor to engage in conversations that can help you identify your right plan.

Maximizing your sobriety also means finding the most meaningful ways to live. For example, if you were accustomed to going to a bar every Friday night, what would now replace this activity? If you engaged in traveling to wineries or breweries, what activity could now give you relaxation and satisfaction? If your friends still partake in these practices, you can choose to spend some time away from influencers who may still want to participate in these pastimes. Explain to friends or family that your current time apart from them is not intended to hurt them but is a way for you to regain clarity so you can have an even better relationship. If they can't understand or support you at this time, it may be time to rethink friendships.

You may also want to assist your sober stages by choosing activities to participate in that you know will help keep you sober and having fun. Choose an inspiring activity or a meeting spot for you and a friend or partner, then go to this place without any anticipation of drinking, even if you would have in your former life. Drinking doesn't need to drive our motivation to complete any task, and the sooner a person learns this, the sooner they can be on their way to celebrating a healthy and long life.

Know Your Worth

I used to think the word power meant having the mental and physical strength to complete any daily obligation. I now see power as a method of progressing toward amazing ideas and innovation. When we think of our true potential and tell ourselves that we deserve the best, we gain the ability to see life in an amazing way. Realizing our worth and potential develops with time and is something that we can experience when we see and feel life clearly. When we understand that we have the ability to change ourselves so we can live the best life imaginable, we start understanding our deeper power.

Take some time to write about what you want to get out of life. Yes, this is a tough idea to consider, but one that will help you realize you're capable of achievement. What would it take for you to live a life you could only imagine? Now, jot down what skills you may need to achieve this life. In many cases, you'll probably realize that you already possess much of the desire to start taking action and that all it would take is more time and money to make this a reality. Well, guess what? You'll have more of by not drinking. You'll now have more time to work on your potential, and you'll save money by no longer drinking alcohol. This is not a race to the end. You have potential and purpose, and when you realize you now have the mental and physical readiness to strive toward a goal with a clearer lens, you'll view your dreams as more achievable.

When you consider how much power and value you have within you to accomplish goals, it's worth sharing your knowledge and motivation with others as well, especially other women. Once you've been on this sober path for some time, serving as a role model for those who are just starting their journey is something that will help increase your worth since you can provide stories and advice for others. Start making notes today about your personal journey so you can one day share these ideas with others and reflect on how far you've come.

Tell yourself each day that you no longer have the time or patience for people who bring you pain. Each action you take should have a purpose in bringing you closer to a goal; otherwise, why do it? Decide what activities and people you value and hold them close. Eliminate the naysayers and events that won't serve you anymore, and find creative, new ways to enjoy your time.

Conclusion

You've heard it before, but changing is hard. When any of us sets out to change something about our lives, it requires motivation and sensitivity. To do this, we have to believe in ourselves and in what we're about to do. The decision to become sober, however, is a low-risk change since it will bring you rewards instead of taking them away. Keep in mind who you want to be and continue staying focused on the goals you set to maintain them. While feeling powerless is one of the hardest feelings, you've learned ways to combat it so that your sobriety is customized for your life. In struggles with relationships, parenting, or career, finding ways to feel power extinguishes any doubt so that we can recognize our potential and value. This then allows us to change, adapt, and move forward, which is something that's nearly impossible when a person still drinks.

For anyone who has gone to AA and has been confronted with the challenge of trying to accept a state of powerlessness before beginning the sober journey, know that this doesn't have to be the start for you. You already possess so much promise just by having the desire to get sober, so use this aptitude as motivation instead. While there are some members of sobriety who take the idea of starting with powerlessness very seriously, the idea of being powerless shouldn't and doesn't need to rule your life. Instead, I ask that you consider what you already bring to the sober table. Have you experienced hurt, defeat, or pain? Do you want to gain sobriety because you feel like this will create a new balance for your future? If so, then you've already been through the worst of something and survived, so you're now in the perfect position to start your journey.

For women, the realization that we have power can give us direction, but this is often a consciousness that comes too late in life because we're not told that we have power from childhood. When we spread the message that all women have the power to make wise choices and love life fully, we remind young girls that their ideas are valued, and they can grow and thrive in a society that won't set them up for failure from the start. When we, as women, give each other persistent and loving encouragement, we set an amazing example for all. Be the model of power that you wish you had growing up. This will make a difference for someone in your future.

Where Are You Now?

If you originally chose to read this book with the intention of someday becoming sober but haven't begun this process yet, consider this day your start. While nothing needs to change this second, know that you already have the power within you to turn your life around by creating a positive structure for yourself. You now have the ability and the template to make your life great, but guess what? You had this potential all along; you simply needed a gentle nudge in the right direction to realize that you've always been strong. In learning to recognize your potential, start speaking up. Begin making confident decisions and listening to yourself instead of others. Every time you do this, your power comes to the surface, and you can take comfort in the fact that you're showing others how influential and impressive you are. Yes, this takes courage, but again, you have had it all along. It's been waiting inside you for this moment.

When I thought long and hard about what would have helped me the most when I first stopped drinking, I remembered an experience I had that might also resonate with you. I was 18 years old and walking down the streets of Manhattan, heading to yet another bar with a group of my friends. I was surrounded by people who I thought I'd know and trust forever. As I walked down the street with these people, though, I still felt an emptiness that no amount of alcohol or drunken discussions with these people could ever fulfill. If I had kept going in this direction, I would surely have placed myself in even more dangerous and harmful situations, and I know that this would have been even more detrimental to my psychological state as well. When I think now about how superficial my relationships with other people were while I was drinking, it makes me feel fortunate that I found sobriety in my life so I could start developing a fearlessness that I would never have had in my teens or early twenties. My point is that I, like many, would never have discovered the benefits of living a sober life had I not taken a chance on myself and made a decision to change. I needed to do this to stop acting like I was living and to start actually living.

If you're still on the fence about starting a sober journey, I offer you this advice: Release what you think you need to do and follow what you know you have to do. In saying this, I realize that there's much work that a person may need to complete to retrain their mind and let go of self-doubt. Know that there are others out there who want to help and speak with you about being your best self, so start finding these invaluable people and support groups today. Online communities and local sobriety groups want nothing more than to offer guidance in helping others gain sobriety, so use these as a resource for your life.

Even if those closest to you don't understand what your goals may be when gaining sobriety, know that you will feel more power and compassion for yourself when you get a new sense of trust that you're doing what's best for you. Never allow someone else's timeline in life to drive your own interpretation of where you are. Your goals can and should be personal to you, so don't limit your thinking by comparing your life or sober journey to someone else's. Starting the journey is what matters most.

Long-Term Investing

There's no way I could be the person I am today if my drinking had continued. This statement is true for me, but it may also sound familiar to others who have maintained their sobriety and reached long-term sobriety milestones in their lives. The benefits that staying sober brings far outweigh the damage of staying locked mentally and physically in a world that makes a person feel sick, dependent, and exhausted. When you set goals for your sober path, you invest in experiences and people in your future. Starting to consider what will make you feel your best means considering what enjoyable activities will keep you moving forward for the long-term. Drinking alcohol only squelches this power and weakens creative ideas.

To change the mind into a place that feels comforting and relaxed is a powerful ability. This helps us find balance and stability each day. We each have this within, but finally, drawing it out by doing what we want to do takes a firm commitment to treat yourself better and with more respect. Once this commitment is made, long-term investing in a sober future can begin, and life can feel as if it's been changed to an elevated state. Keep this in mind as you consider your next steps. This trip in life is yours, and you can do whatever you choose. If you're at a standstill, waiting for something to fall into your lap, you may be waiting forever. If you take action now to personalize a powerful plan for yourself, you're likely to see benefits in a short amount of time. Decide to respect the person you know is inside of you because you are deserving of it. Tell yourself each day that you can and will feel powerful because you now know how. You have the instruments you need to make your life beautiful, so you can begin now.

When I realized how to recognize my power, I was then able to motivate myself to feel empowered each day. Realizing this helped in every aspect of my life, from my work to my personal life. It then helped as I got older and watched my kids grow, my family change and sober friendships thrived. When I think about the wonderful people in my life now who I trust and value so greatly, I know I wouldn't be this powerful without them. We fuel the power within each other when we share our stories and victories in our lives.

The amazing discoveries you can make through sobriety will open new doors and take you in incredible directions that you probably never planned for. As a new friend and sobriety advocate, I'm here on the sidelines rooting for you, so use this day to discover something powerful inside you. You have the power and can succeed. Never doubt this again.

References

About the national sexual assault telephone hotline. (2000). RAINN. https://www.rainn.org/about-national-sexual-assault-telephone-hotline

Alcohol and the brain: An overview. (2022). National institute on alcohol abuse and alcoholism (NIAAA). https://www.niaaa.nih.gov/publications/alcohol-and-brain-overview#:~:text=Alcohol%20interferes%20with%20the%20brain%27s

Azab, M. (2020, June 9). *The brain under the influence of power.* Psychologytoday.com. https://www.psychologytoday.com/us/blog/neuroscience-in-everyday-life/202006/the-brain-under-the-influence-power

The big book. (n.d.). *Alcoholics anonymous.* https://www.aa.org/the-big-book

Boitnott, J. (2014, September 16). *Get over it: 5 strategies for pushing past failure.* Inc.com. https://www.inc.com/john-boitnott/get-over-it-5-strategies-for-pushing-past-failure.html

Bradberry, T. (2016, June 16). *11 habits that make people seek power.* World Economic Forum. https://www.weforum.org/agenda/2016/06/why-do-peope-want-power/

Bradford Health Services. (2023, March 22). *4 types of boundaries in recovery.* Bradford Health Services. https://bradfordhealth.com/4-types-of-boundaries-in-recovery/

Brain recovery after alcohol abuse. (n.d.). Lifeworkscommunity. Retrieved May 11, 2023, from https://www.lifeworkscommunity.com/blog/how-long-does-brain-recovery-take-after-alcohol-abuse#:~:text=Once%20an%20alcoholic%20has%20stopped

Clear, J. (2012, December 31). *Identity-based habits: How to actually stick to your goals this year.* James Clear. https://jamesclear.com/identity-based-habits

Drinking too much alcohol can harm your health. Learn the facts. (2020, April 23). . Centers for Disease Control and Prevention. https://www.cdc.gov/alcohol/fact-sheets/alcohol-use.htm#:~:text=Long%2DTerm%20Health%20Risks

DuRivage-Jacobs, S. (2022, March 8). *A brief history of women in alcohol recovery: A look at the last 200+ years.* Join Tempest. https://jointempest.com/resources/womens-recovery-movement/

Editorial Staff. (2023, January 20). *How are emotional effects of alcohol explained?* Alcohol.org. https://alcohol.org/guides/alcohol-fueled-emotions/

8 benefits of a sober living program for women. (2023, February 21). Women's Recovery. https://www.womensrecovery.com/womens-rehab-blog/8-reasons-sober-woman-will-change-life-better/

Fountain, T. M. (2020, October 20). *Council post: Seven outstanding ways to overcome failure and succeed.* Forbes. https://www.forbes.com/sites/forbesbusinesscouncil/2020/10/20/seven-outstanding-ways-to-overcome-failure-and-succeed/?sh=47f782904200

Frakt, A., & Carroll, A. E. (2020, March 11). *Alcoholics anonymous vs. other approaches: The evidence is now in.* The New York Times. https://www.nytimes.com/2020/03/11/upshot/alcoholics-anonymous-new-evidence.html

Glaser, G. (2015, March 17). *The Irrationality of alcoholics anonymous.* The Atlantic.

https://www.theatlantic.com/magazine/archive/2015/04/the-irrationality-of-alcoholics-anonymous/386255/

Guarnotta, E. (2022, April 12). *What makes alcoholics anonymous (AA) successful?* GoodRx. https://www.goodrx.com/conditions/alcohol-use-disorder/what-makes-aa-successful

History of AA (n.d.). *Alcoholics anonymous.* https://www.aa.org/aa-history

Ibarra, H., Ely, R., & Kolb, D. (2013, September). *Women rising: The unseen barriers.* Harvard Business Review. https://hbr.org/2013/09/women-rising-the-unseen-barriers

Koob, G. F., & White, A. (2022, May 6). *Neuroscience: The brain in addiction and recovery. National institute on alcohol abuse and alcoholism (NIAAA).* https://www.niaaa.nih.gov/health-professionals-communities/core-resource-on-alcohol/neuroscience-brain-addiction-and-recovery

Koss, M. P. (2022, June 13). *Alcohol is becoming more common in sexual assault among college students.* The Conversation. https://theconversation.com/alcohol-is-becoming-more-common-in-sexual-assault-among-college-students-171584

LaPierre, J. (n.d.). *Alcoholics anonymous for atheists.* Choose Help. https://www.choosehelp.com/topics/alcoholism/aa-for-atheists-2013-how-to-take-what-you-need-and-leave-the-rest

MacFarlane, K. (2021, December 16). *5 myths about sobriety.* Recovery Elevator. https://www.recoveryelevator.com/5-myths-about-sobriety-from-alcohol/

Manwarren Generes, W. (Ed.). (2023, April 19). *How to get sober: A guide to sobriety.* American Addiction Centers. https://americanaddictioncenters.org/sobriety-guide

The Maryland Collaborative. (2016). *Sexual assault and alcohol: what the research evidence tells us recognize the complexity of the association.* Nida.nih. https://nida.nih.gov/sites/default/files/sexualassault.pdf

Mayo Clinic Staff. (2020, August 18). *Exercise and stress: Get moving to manage stress*. Mayo Clinic. https://www.mayoclinic.org/healthy-lifestyle/stress-management/in-depth/exercise-and-stress/art-20044469#:~:text=Exercise%20increases%20your%20overall%20health

McPherson, G. (2022, November 3). *Your brain could be stopping you from breaking bad habits*. KLTN. https://www.klkntv.com/your-brain-could-be-stopping-your-from-breaking-bad-habits/

Nicole, A. (2019, August 22). *3 kind, simple & effective ways to communicate your boundaries*. Medium. https://headway.ginger.io/3-kind-simple-effective-ways-to-communicate-your-boundaries-46dad0989e79

Office of Women's Health. (n.d.). *Effects of violence against women | Office on women's health*. Womenshealth.gov. Retrieved May 11, 2023, from https://www.womenshealth.gov/relationships-and-safety/effects-violence-against-women#:~:text=Other%20effects%20can%20include%20shutting

Raypole, C. (2020, October 19). *How to stop drinking: 14 tips for success*. Healthline. https://www.healthline.com/health/alcohol/how-to-stop-drinking#go-deep

The Recovery Village. (2022, May 6). *The top seven ways getting sober will change your life (in a good way)*. (J. Strum, Ed.). The Recovery Village Drug and Alcohol Rehab. https://www.therecoveryvillage.com/recovery/sober-living/top-ways-sobriety-changes-life/

Rigby, A. (n.d.). *The five types of power (and how you can wield them like a superhero)*. Fingerprintforsuccess.com. https://www.fingerprintforsuccess.com/blog/types-of-power

Simmons, R. (n.d.). *Everyone fails. Here's how to pick yourself back up*. Nytimes.com. https://www.nytimes.com/guides/working-womans-handbook/how-to-overcome-failure

Stevens, K. (Ed.). (2023, January 6). *Step 1 of alcoholics anonymous | Step 1 aa.* Alcohol.org. https://alcohol.org/alcoholics-anonymous/step-1/

Substance Abuse and Mental Health Services Administration (US Office of the Surgeon General). (2016, November). *Recovery: The many paths to wellness.* US Department of Health and Human Services. https://www.ncbi.nlm.nih.gov/books/NBK424846/

T, B. (2022a, March 8). *The benefits of quitting alcohol.* Verywell Mind. https://www.verywellmind.com/what-are-the-benefits-of-alcohol-recovery-67761

T, B. (2022b, September 17). *7 tips for staying clean and sober.* Verywell Mind. https://www.verywellmind.com/tips-for-staying-clean-and-sober-67900

Tartakovsky, M. (2021, August 19). *8 approaches to find yourself.* Psych Central. https://psychcentral.com/health/ways-to-get-to-know-yourself-better#what-now

Thalwal, R. (2022, January 9). *3 powerful steps to set-up your boundaries to live in peace.* Change Your Mind Change Your Life. https://medium.com/change-your-mind/3-powerful-steps-to-set-up-your-boundaries-to-live-in-peace-4f8a15b6fefc

Understanding alcohol use disorder. (2021). National Institute on Alcohol Abuse and Alcoholism. https://www.niaaa.nih.gov/publications/brochures-and-fact-sheets/understanding-alcohol-use-disorder

Why is it so hard for us to ask for help? (2020, January 24). Steps Recovery Center. https://www.stepsrc.com/why-is-it-so-hard-for-us-to-ask-for-help/

Women for sobriety. (n.d.). Women for Sobriety. https://womenforsobriety.org/

Made in the USA
Las Vegas, NV
03 September 2023